The Genius to Improve an Invention

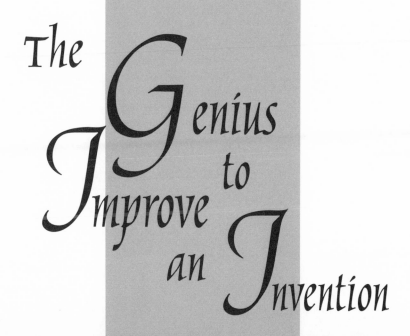

The Genius to Improve an Invention

Literary Transitions

PIERO BOITANI

UNIVERSITY OF NOTRE DAME PRESS

Notre Dame, Indiana

Copyright © 2002 by
University of Notre Dame
Notre Dame, Indiana 46556
http://www.undpress.nd.edu

Manufactured in the United States of America

Originally published in 1999 as
Il genio di migliorare un'invenzione: transizioni letterarie
(Bologna: Il Mulino).

Library of Congress Cataloging-in-Publication Data
Boitani, Piero.
[Genio di migliorare un'invenzione. English]
The genius to improve an invention : literary transitions /
Piero Boitani.
p. cm.
Includes bibliographical references and index.
ISBN 0-268-02950-4 (cloth : alk. paper)
ISBN 0-268-02951-2 (pbk. : alk. paper)
1. Literature, Comparative. 2. Literature—History and criticism.
I. Title.
PN875 .B6513   2002
809—dc21   2002009384

for *P*_{AT}

Contents

Preface to
the American Edition

The "genius to improve an invention" is Dryden's phrase for the very British tendency to borrow literary texts from the past and "perfect" them. The English, he states, are incapable of "inventing" anything, limiting themselves to improving on other people's inventions—an accusation abundantly levelled by the West at the Japanese, as I was smilingly informed in Tokyo recently. Dryden himself of course offers, as we see in chapter 3, numerous examples of "improvement," particularly in those *Fables* in the preface to which the phrase appears.

"Improvement" obviously lies in the eye of successive beholders, but I have always suspected that the word also implied some idea of that species of literary transmission which comes somewhere between T. S. Eliot's notion of tradition and the individual talent and Harold Bloom's "anxiety of influence." "Improving" means kicking against ancestorly traces, of course, but it also means accepting our predecessors, taking them on in a nonbelligerent sense—indeed, positively loving them with filial devotion: a relationship which will inevitably be (as Bloom argues) Oedipal-Freudian but also a special one of affection and "moving beyond." A classic compromise, in short, not without a grain of hypocrisy and a good dose of English common sense: hence my decision to end each of the following chapters with a work from English literature.

"Improving," to use the paradigm of scientific revolutions, means making the necessary adjustments to the model in order to "save appearances" (the "phenomena") and make them tally with current data; then, when it is no longer convenient, or economical, to improve on the model, it gets radically changed, revolutionised. The history of Western literature, like the evolution of the human species, is made up of infinite improvements, very few huge leaps, and a welter of steps backward. Some of the changes are epoch making and in part constitute, or at least reflect, cultural, social, and political revolutions of the first order; others simply reflect the personality and tastes of an individual author.

In his *Electra,* as we see in chapter 1, Euripides coolly strips off Aeschylus's model of recognition—nothing less than the process of the acquisition of knowledge. Intended to be revolutionary, this ultimately, however, becomes a return to the past. Sophocles, on the other hand, is content with improving the model through a series of phenomenal inventions, and for the next two thousand years drama will continue to improve them until they finally disappear. It is Shakespeare, in *Hamlet,* who subverts them once and for all. In *Troilus and Criseyde,* Chaucer improves on Boccaccio's *Filostrato* with the assistance of Boethius, Guinizzelli, and Dante. He is no revolutionary but an English reformist of some genius. If this little group had an arsonist, it was Dante, linking Francesca to Beatrice in a reinterpretation of his own poetic development and the whole "cor gentile" culture. In the same way, in the story of Palamon and Arcite, the Boccaccio of the *Teseida* "invents," Chaucer improves, Shakespeare and Fletcher ignite, and Dryden returns to Chaucer for a thorough makeover. T. S. Eliot adores Dante and re-creates him. In the tragedy of blindness, however, Oedipus and Lear, although reduced to near-identical nothingness, have almost nothing in common. Lear simply ignores Oedipus's scientific and rational enquiry, his search for cognition, and can re-cognize only through madness.

What I shall be looking at in the book, then, is the problem of literary *transition* in its wider sense, as a metamorphosis of stories, themes, characters, and imagery: of the transformations they undergo in passing from one author to another, from one country's literature to another's, from one period to another. It goes without saying that transition is the basis of comparative studies and the basis of *European* or Western literature— the only one I can read with any degree of precision. This is the reason I begin and end, "framing" the book, by looking through a telescope at a series of texts from antiquity to the modern age. My frame chapters take the question of anagnorisis—agnition as the central element of the "complex" plot, in Aristotle's codification—as the point of departure for an exploration of recognition as a problem of knowledge (and not abstract knowledge but a process bred in the bone of specific individuals) in a number of works of literature. What is analysed, of course, is not only literature, but, in its different manifestations, the development of Western gnoseology (the "reasoning" of Electra and Hamlet; Oedipus's enquiry and the recognition which grows "from the events themselves" in Sophocles and in *King Lear*).

The ideal epigraph for these two sections and for the whole work is perhaps a statement of Socrates in Plato's *Theaetetus* (193c) which refers very clearly to the recognition scene in Aeschylus's *Choephoroi*. It evokes the image of the soul as a tablet of wax on which all knowledge is impressed like the mark of a seal but is also an overall view of the scientist's and the philosopher's work:

> We are left with the possibility of judging what is false in the following case. I know you [Theaetetus] and Theodorus, and have imprints of the two of you on that piece of wax, like those of signet rings. I see you both, some way off and not properly, and I am eager to assign the imprint which belongs to each to the seeing which belongs to each, and to insert and fit the seeing into its own trace, so that recognition may take place. But, missing that aim, and making a transposition, I attach the seeing of each to the imprint which belongs to the other, like people who put their shoes on the wrong feet; or alternatively my going wrong is because the same sort of thing happens to me as happens to sight in mirrors, when it flows in such a way as to transpose left and right. It is then that different-judging and the making of false judgements occur.

I would also take this as a wonderful metaphor for the work of the critic. Criticism, it seems to me, is but a humble and exalting piece of recognition. When it goes wrong, putting the wrong shoes on the wrong feet or looking at mere mirror images, criticism runs the risk of making *pseudē*—false judgements—and of becoming what Plato calls *heterodoxia*: "different-judging," mistaken reading, confused interpretation. My aim here is to show the reader a series of possible paths toward anagnorisis.

To go back to my plot: There is no direct source connection between the different works in the first and last chapters, apart from the Electra sequence from Aeschylus, Euripides, and Sophocles down to Voltaire,

Alfieri, Hofmannsthal, Sartre, O'Neill, Lowell, and Yourcenar. The connection grows out of situation, scene, and theme, so that Electra and Hamlet, for example, share the *syllogismos,* the reasoning, the deduction, the syllogistic logic; Oedipus and Lear, recognition and nothingness. But I also believe that literary transmission, Dryden's "improving," is also to a great extent this resurfacing of scene and theme in a constant reworking of myths (as Aristotle was well aware); an intertextual rather than philological echoing through space and time. For this reason, in that they subsume considerably more comprehensive issues, I have used these two chapters to begin and end the work. And in this sense the present volume constitutes a complement to my earlier work on rewriting, a sequence—in the realm of "secular" literature—to what I called *re-Scriptures* in *The Bible and Its Rewritings.*

In chapters 2, 3, and 4 the telescope becomes a microscope, albeit concentrated on whole tissue samples rather than single cells. Here the works are directly interlinked, as endorsed either by philology or the authors themselves. Dante's Francesca and Chaucer's Criseyde (and Troilus) have a number of things in common but one above all, announced in the title of chapter 2: Guinizzelli's great poem "Al cor gentile rempaira sempre amore." And to read this through Dante's and Chaucer's eyes means exploring the various transformations of "courtly love," travelling through death and sublimation, the Inferno, Purgatory, and Paradise, and hunting down the haunts of God.

In the third chapter, which gives the volume its title, the sequence is exclusively English, after Boccaccio's Italian prelude: Chaucer—Shakespeare-cum-Fletcher—Dryden. Here, too, the dimensions are decidedly wide-screen—love, both hetero and homo, bestiality, destiny, and God—but gradually exposed through minute details and vital if near imperceptible improvements: the doubling of scenes, the reinvention of characters, plots, similarities, and single lines or words, all clues to much more significant changes of authorial viewpoint, belief system, and episteme.

Chapter 4, in anticipation of the book's conclusions, returns to the question of recognition, from the splendid, tragic, pathos-shot scene between Brunetto and Dante to the ambiguous, painful, but eventually fruitful meeting between the protagonist, the "I" of T. S. Eliot's *Four Quartets,* and the "familiar compound ghost" of *Little Gidding* II, explicitly modelled on *Inferno* XV. Here the microscope is used again but for more general purposes: to compare two techniques and periods, the fourteenth and twentieth centuries, and two poets, the modern one the self-declared "son" of his medieval "father," within their very different cultural paradigms.

General conclusions I have left to the reader. I offer summaries and sketch in contexts of the works I examine only when strictly necessary, but I analyse single episodes and scenes in considerable textual and contextual detail, with ample use of quotation. Nothing more than the text itself, which has its own peculiar "voice" and intonation (even in translation), makes clear the critic's argument and points the way to individual reading. By a similar logic, nothing irritates a passionate, serious reader more than notes. Hence, I have given simply a brief bibliography with the points of reference I considered essential for myself. After all, any reader worth her or his salt will possess the genius to improve the invention of the author.

·   ·   ·

The debts I have incurred in composing and rewriting a book such as the present one are numberless, because it has taken me a fair amount of time, and quite an amount of moving from place to place, to focus on this project. Many years ago, in Rome and Cambridge, Mario Praz and Jack Bennett taught me to embark on short and long journeys through more than one literature. But I cannot forget that Patrick Boyde has been pointing out to me, for more than thirty years now, the way of precision, clarity, and concreteness. To him, therefore, in friendship, I dedicate this book in the first place. On particular themes I have been helped, directly or indirectly, by Muriel Bradbrook, Hans-Jürgen Diller, Peter Dronke, Donald and Sara Maddox, Pamela and David Benson, Douglas Gray, Barry Windeatt, Karl-Heinz Göller, and Guido Almansi. Jill Mann's sharp mind has been present to me, whether in the fore- or background, ever since I began to think of a volume like this, and it is of course not by chance that the book, which was conceived in Cambridge more than twenty years ago, now sees the light in Notre Dame. Without her and without Michael Lapidge, Maura Nolan, Dan Blanton, Christian Moevs, Martin Bloomer, and above all Ted and Annamaria Cachey, I would probably never have set foot in the wild plains of Indiana, and certainly not survived them. In this last respect, I also owe a lot to Alessandro Guerra Pedrazzi, Lisa Caponigri, and Sharon Konopka.

This American edition would have been impossible without the courtesy and help of Barbara Hanrahan.

The linguistic vicissitudes of the book are part of the fun it has been to write it. Originally conceived and written in English, these chapters were translated into Italian by Marina Peri and published by Il Mulino. But in preparing the Italian edition, I could not refrain from adding, changing, cutting, rewriting—in short, from "improving"—the original invention. What I present here is, for all but the last chapter, the pristine English text (which I could not have recovered without the help of Emilia Di Rocco), "fortified"—as Dryden would put it—for a new audience, and modified to take into account the Italian version as well as further "improvements." Since I was not satisfied with my English original of chapter 5, I have asked Anita Weston to translate it anew from the Italian and have subsequently rewritten her text. In sum, I do not quite know in what language I am writing, but I trust the ingenuity of American readers enough to hope that they will understand it.

PIERO BOITANI
Rome, Easter 2001

CHAPTER ONE

Electra and Hamlet

Recognition and Reasoning

Electra and Hamlet are no doubt two of the greatest tragic characters in
Western literature. Part of their success in the European tradition may
well be owing to the fact that they show recognition as intimately connected with the exercise of their rational faculties. Here, I examine this
connection in the light of Aristotle's discussion of recognition in the
Poetics.

For Aristotle, recognition (anagnorisis) constitutes, together with
peripeteia (reversal) and *pathos* (catastrophe), a key element of both the
tragic and the epic plot. It generates pity and fear (*eleos* and *phobos*),
which is the purpose of the mimesis inherent in tragedy, and it produces
a "shock" of surprise and emotion tied to wonder. It is—thus his own
definition—"a change from ignorance to knowledge" (*gnosis*), and although this knowledge is of a particular person (or at times an object
or an event), yet, because in his view poetry is more "philosophical" than
history and is concerned with universals, the knowledge that recognition leads us to is, it can be inferred, universal. Several combinations of
ignorance, knowledge, error (*hamartia*), and anagnorisis, as well as several forms of anagnorisis, are possible. Indeed some critics have seen in
the list of types of recognitions that Aristotle gives us in chapter 16 of
the *Poetics* a mirror of the ascending kinds of knowledge—senses, memory, intellect, and "intuition"—he describes in the *Metaphysics*, as well
as a correspondence with the various "elements" of tragedy—stage spec-
tacle, "thought," and mythos—propounded in the *Poetics* itself (for

instance, recognition "through memory" and "through reasoning" belong
to the sphere of imagination and rational thinking and can be considered as parts of the inner "thought" of a play). In the *Poetics* we have, in
ascending order: (1) recognition through signs, *sēmeia,* both natural (a
birthmark) and acquired, the latter either on the body (scars) or external (rings, necklaces, etc.); (2) recognition through memory (Odysseus
is recognized by Alcynous when he weeps at the bard's singing of Troy);
(4) recognition based on reasoning (what Aristotle calls *syllogismos*), with
its parallel type, based on mistaken inference on the part of the audience (*paralogismos tou theatrou*); and best of all (5) recognition which
arises from the events themselves and coincides with *peripeteia* (*Oedipus Rex* is the model).

   In fact, Aristotle quotes as a typical example of anagnorisis *ek syllo-
gismou* the recognition scene between Electra and Orestes in Aeschylus's
Choephoroi (458 B.C.E.). After Aeschylus gave it a unique pattern and significance, this scene seems to have had central importance in Greek culture and to have occupied the best minds of Athens in discussions the
issue of which concerns not only drama but science and philosophy as
well. If we accept the modern datings of post-Aeschylean Electra plays,
Euripides' tragedy, which contains a deliberate artistic and philosophical attack upon Aeschylus's scene, goes back to ca. 418 B.C.E., whereas
Sophocles' version, which seems to take up a middle ground between
Aeschylus and Euripides, would belong to the years around 413 B.C.E.
In 423–422 Aristophanes mentions Aeschylus's scene in *The Clouds.* We
do not know how he would have considered Euripides' version, but judg-
ing from the treatment he receives in the *Frogs* (405 B.C.E.), we may pre-
sume that Aristophanes would have pronounced a pretty severe sentence
on the Euripidean *Electra.*

   Debate of the Electra scene by dramatists in their plays thus covers
the second half of the fifth century B.C.E., the age of Pericles, sophism,
and Socrates. In the two immediately following generations, philosophers
resume the discussion, and once more this focuses on Aeschylus's version, to which Plato alludes in his *Theaetetus* and which Aristotle chooses
as paradigmatic of anagnorisis "through reasoning" in the *Poetics.*

   Why does there grow in classical Greece so much interest for a
single, apparently minor scene of drama? My answer to this question is
threefold. In the first place, the importance of the Electra-Orestes recog-

nition in a play about Orestes' return home and his revenge of his father Agamemnon's murder upon his mother Clytemnestra and her lover Aegisthus is absolutely fundamental. The moment in which Electra, who alone in the Atreid family has kept faith with the memory of her father, recognises her brother Orestes marks the turning point in the action of such a play, where the union of brother and sister alone can bring about the completion of divinely ordained revenge (nemesis) within the justice of the *lex talionis*. In Aeschylus's Oresteian trilogy, which begins with Agamemnon's return and his murder and ends with Orestes being acquitted of his matricide by the "new" justice of Athens, the recognition scene corresponds to the first reversal, or *peripeteia*, in the plot of the tragedy.

Second, that recognition scene stands at the end of a return, Orestes', implicitly contrasted with Agamemnon's *nostos*, where reunion between husband and wife spelt death to the former. The recognition between Electra and Orestes fulfils a strong expectation, reunites brother and sister, reconstructs a family—a "house" now divided, fragmented, and dispersed—reestablishes the "old" order and opens the way to justice.

Finally, the technical means employed by each playwright to effect the anagnorisis have a bearing on the artistic construction of each play and imply different gnoseological and epistemological attitudes, in particular with regard to the value of signs and "reasoning."

The three fundamental moments in the story of Orestes' revenge must be his return, the recognition with Electra, and the murder of Clytemnestra and Aegisthus: there is no way in which the order and logic of this *mythos* can be changed without in fact constructing a wholly new story, with a different meaning. Aristotle proclaims this aloud in the *Poetics*. But he maintains—thus revealing himself as the first theorist of *the genius to improve an invention*—that a poet has the right and the duty to "manage transmitted stories well, in an artistic manner": "It is not admissible to alter traditional stories, the murder of Clytemnestra by Orestes, for instance, and that of Eriphyle by Alcmaeon; on the other hand, the poet must use his imagination and handle the traditional material effectively." The plots of the Electra plays by Aeschylus, Euripides, and Sophocles bear witness to the "constrained freedom" with which a Greek playwright can treat his themes. Aeschylus places the recognition scene almost at the beginning of the *Choephoroi*; Euripides has it one-third of the way through his *Electra;* and Sophocles delays to the final third of the play. Three clearly different dramatic strategies inspire these changes of tempo, as will be apparent from a consideration of the three plays' scale and emphasis.

The *Choephoroi,* just over a thousand lines in length, runs its course from beginning to middle and end without superfluous episodes and stages essentially one active character, Orestes. Electra disappears from the play once the revenge proper starts, the function of the nurse is simply that of calling Aegisthus back to the Palace, and Pylades pronounces only one, though decisive, sentence (when Orestes hesitates to kill his mother, his friend replies to his question whether he should with, "Where then are Apollo's words? What becomes of man's sworn oaths?"). In Euripides, the play has become more than thirteen hundred lines long, Orestes and Electra kill their mother together, Pylades is silent throughout, but we have a peasant (Electra's husband), a messenger (who describes Aegisthus's death), and an old man who had been Agamemnon's guardian and who recognizes Orestes, and finally two *dei ex machina,* the Dioscuri. With Sophocles, *Electra* has become a play of fifteen hundred lines, with a series of secondary episodes that make the plot "complex." The theme of Orestes' death, already present in Aeschylus (and absent in Euripides), is amplified, the supposedly tragic end of the hero being first announced by the old man and then apparently confirmed by Orestes and Pylades, who carry on stage the urn which we are told contains Orestes' ashes. Finally, the main characters have increased to include Electra's sister, Chrysothemis, to whom it now falls to find the lock of hair by Agamemnon's tomb.

Aeschylus's plot underlines the problem which is central for him, that of justice. Clytemnestra has murdered Agamemnon, blood calls for blood, Apollo has ordered Orestes to exact revenge. Accordingly, with but one hesitation, the hero proceeds with his task. The "middle" of the play, significantly, is taken up by the long dialogue in which Orestes, Electra, and the Chorus discuss *dikē,* or justice, evoke the past of the Atreid family and Agamemnon's murder, pray for his assistance, and learn of Clytemnestra's dream (in which she gives birth to a serpent that sucks clots of blood together with her milk). The end of the play leaves the central question open once more. As soon as Orestes has killed his mother, he is in turn "polluted" and the Furies start tormenting him. The anagnorisis between Electra and Orestes, which comes very early in this plot, is not only instrumental to the revenge, it reconstructs the "eagle's blood bereaved," the *domos*, the House around which the entire trilogy revolves.

In Euripides, Electra is much more prominent, and the whole play has a more "pathetic" setting. Electra's ruthlessness in exacting revenge, like her mother's murder of Agamemnon, has personal motivations as well as the general ones of justice. She has been banished from her father's house, turned into a peasant's wife. Above all, as Clytemnestra tells her, anticipating the formulation of Freud's "Electra complex," her nature has always been to love her father. The question of justice, therefore, is much more individual: should Orestes and his sister kill their mother? The ideal centre of the play has Electra and her brother discuss this, with Orestes, anguished at the thought, maintaining that matricide is wrong and that perhaps a fiend disguised as Apollo commanded him to kill Clytemnestra. The solution to Orestes' and Electra's dilemma comes at the end of the play with the Dioscuri—Castor and Pollux, Clytemnestra's divine brothers—announcing Orestes' acquittal by the Athenian tribunal. Apollo will take upon himself the blame for Clytemnestra's death. His "unwise" prophecy and Fate are responsible for the matricide. Yet this answer is, clearly, not satisfying, for it raises another crucial question left unanswered here: can one trust the gods? In this thematic context, the recognition between Orestes and Electra, even more essential here than in Aeschylus for the progress of the action, acquires a different light. Celebrated by Electra as the first "victory" the "god" is bringing them, the reunion between brother and sister, pathetic as it is, represents but a short-lived personal joy. The House of the Atreids is not at all rebuilt, and it is interesting to notice that in the last scene of the play Orestes and Electra weep at length over the separation imposed on them by Castor and Pollux. The thread joining that anagnorisis and coming together with this final parting is indeed emblematic of the play's situation and message.

The very curious thing about Sophocles' *Electra* is the apparently minor part played in it by the revenge proper. Both Clytemnestra and Aegisthus are killed in just over one hundred lines at the end of the play. Furthermore, in contrast with both Aeschylus's and Euripides' versions, Clytemnestra is murdered before Aegisthus, and neither Orestes nor Electra seems to show any hesitation before the matricide. Finally, there seems to be no hint of the crucial problem arising from Orestes' killing of his mother—the problem represented by the Furies in Aeschylus and by the message of the Dioscuri in Euripides.

In the *Choephoroi,* the protagonist is Orestes, at least for the last two-thirds of the play. In Euripides, Orestes and Electra are both central figures and both kill their mother. Sophocles undoubtedly makes Electra the true protagonist of most of his play. She is alone, anguished by her misery and debasement, full of resentment toward Clytemnestra and Aegisthus, relentless for revenge, ready to perform it on her own. Yet the punishment of Clytemnestra and Aegisthus is not just the fruit of Electra's fury. Sophocles keeps the deep motivation of Aeschylus's play. Electra replies to Clytemnestra with perfect logic: "Should [Agamemnon] have died at your hand? By what law? Watch out lest in setting up this law for mortals you set up pain and remorse for yourself. For if we kill one man in retaliation for another, you would be the first to die if you meet justice." The House and the dead are similarly active in the accomplishment of justice. As Clytemnestra is being killed, the Chorus exclaims, "O city, o race, unhappy, now your fate of every day is wasting away, wasting away . . . the curses fulfil. Those who lie below the earth live, for the long dead drain their killers' blood, flowing in retribution." There is, however, something out of joint (and I think deliberately so) in this logic. I shall give only two indications of this. Clytemnestra, who declares herself "not conscience-stricken" at Agamemnon's murder, feels very uncertain when she learns that Orestes is dead: "What am I to say of these things? Am I to call them fortunate, or terrible, but beneficial? . . . [I]t is an awesome thing to be a mother. Even when you suffer despite at their hands, you cannot hate those you bore." At the end of the play, the Chorus and Electra listen to Clytemnestra's cries as she is being murdered. When Orestes hits her for the first time, Electra exclaims, "Strike if you have strength, a second blow." But there is no doubt that, both before and after this, the Chorus expresses all its horror at what is being done: "I heard a cry that should never have been heard—I shudder." Only a few lines later, when Orestes and Pylades have killed Clytemnestra, the Chorus seems to recant. "I cannot fault them," it says. This oscillation (which would be crystallized at line 423 if, with the manuscripts, we read *legein,* "I can say nothing") is typical of the kind of play Sophocles has written. When, in the last sentence, the Chorus comments, "O seed of Atreus, how, having suffered much, you have finally made your way to liberty, perfected as you are by this onset," we ask ourselves what exactly this means. What "freedom" is the Chorus talking about? And what kind of "fulfilment" or "perfection" (*teleothen*) has the *sperma*—the "seed"—of Atreus achieved?

We are, I think, meant to ask these questions. Sophocles' *Electra* is a "problem" play. Let us consider the structure of the plot. The revenge, we have seen, is reduced to two brief scenes at the end. The recognition between Orestes and Electra is delayed to the last third of the play. In fact, the whole "middle" of *Electra* is taken up by what I would call a "recognition plot." This begins with the arrival of the old man who announces and describes in splendidly epic detail Orestes' death in the races at Delphi. In lines 755–56, interestingly enough exactly halfway through the 1,510 lines of the play, the theme is brought to sudden focus by the old man's words. After his fall from the chariot, Orestes was dragged by the horses in the dust. He was so stained by blood "that none of his *philoi* [his "friends" and "relations"] would have recognized him by looking at the wretched corpse." Indeed, his body was immediately cremated and his ashes placed in the urn that Electra "recognizes" as Orestes' when, accompanied by Orestes himself, it appears onstage. Meanwhile, Chrysotemis reports her finding the lock of hair, the "sign" (*tekmērion*) of the Aeschylean anagnorisis. Electra discards this, in favour of the "sign" (*tekmēria*) represented by the urn. Slowly, this evidence is proved false and Agamemnon's signet ring becomes the "sign" of the true recognition. Finally, more than one hundred lines later, the old man is recognized by Electra as the "paidagogos" who saved Orestes after Agamemnon's death.

I shall return to this recognition plot presently. For the moment, I note only that it introduces into the play the notion that reality can be ambiguous, that truth may be hidden behind it, and that recognition is a process which might have to retrace its steps through *méconnaissance*. And this is precisely what both Clytemnestra and Aegisthus have to learn, too. If the recognition plot marks the "middle" of the play and its climax, the Electra-Orestes anagnorisis sets the *peripeteia* in motion, and the "end" of the play sees *peripeteia* coinciding with a double recognition. As she prepares the fatal urn for the funeral rites, Clytemnestra discovers, in a dreadful flash, that one of the men standing behind her is Orestes: "Son, son, have pity on her who gave you birth!" Anagnorisis explodes into matricide as the mute urn reveals the perfect emptiness of "things." Soon after, Aegisthus returns unaware to the palace and wants "proof" that Orestes is dead. He asks Orestes and Pylades to raise the veil which covers the corpse lying before him, believing it to be Orestes', and would have Clytemnestra summoned. As Orestes replies, "She is close. Do not look for her elsewhere," Aegisthus raises the veil and exclaims, "Alas, what do I see?" "Whom do you fear, whom do you not recognize?" asks Orestes cruelly, and while Aegisthus is still uncertain about the identity of his enemy he adds, "Are you not aware that you have been addressing living men as if they were dead?" Finally, Aegisthus recognizes Orestes. Thus revenge is made to concur with anagnorisis, "justice" is accomplished at the same time as truth and reality are unveiled, and recognition dominates the play, inviting the audience to acquire true knowledge of its tragic meaning.

Let us now return to the recognition mechanisms employed by the three poets to see how they work and what they mean. The three scenes have two elements in common: the finding of the lock of hair (by Electra in Aeschylus, by the old man in Euripides, by Chrysotemis in Sophocles) and the ultimate proof of Orestes' identity by means of a material sign (Electra's piece of weaving in the *Choephoroi*, the scar on Orestes' brow in Euripides, Agamemnon's signet ring in Sophocles). In all three versions, these two elements are closely linked to each other. They are both "signs," albeit (and here is the rub, as we shall see) of a different nature, and the "acquired" sign—as Aristotle would call the vestment, the ring, and the scar—always follows the "inherited" sign (the lock of hair). Also, while the cloth, the scar, and the ring are purely "material," impersonal signs, the lock of hair has a "personal" value (it comes from Orestes' own head by an act of his will) and a "ritual" significance, which ties it to the roots of the tragedy (it is placed on Agamemnon's tomb as a sacrifice to his memory). The two kinds of signs are, then, clearly charged with a different intensity and occupy a different position in the plot of the three plays.

Aeschylus gives particular prominence to the "inherited" sign by making Electra find it and use it to initiate an anguished discussion with the Chorus and with herself. Here we have three main stages. In the first, Electra sees the lock and, reasoning by exclusion, concludes that Orestes has sent it. The scheme of this *syllogismos* is as follows. Electra: I see a lock. Chorus: Whose can it be? Electra: None but myself would make this offering; it is very likely *our* own. Chorus: Can it be that Orestes offered it? Electra: It resembles *his*. Chorus: But how did he venture to

come here? Electra rightly concludes: he has *sent* it. Behind the impeccable form, the logic playing in the argument responds to the inner nature
of the sign by progressing from *me* to *us* and *him*—in other words, by
moving from personal identity to family connotation and finally to the
brother's person in a parabola from particular to species and again to
the individual.

At this point, Electra launches into an anguished monologue, itself
divided into two sections. In the first, she balances out the possibilities:
"How can I expect someone else to own this lock? My mother did not
shear it from her head. But how can I assent it is Orestes'?" "My mind
is divided." This meditation culminates in a cry at the muteness of the
signs themselves: "If only this lock, like a messenger, had a kindly voice
to set my mind at rest!" In the second part of the monologue Electra finds
the footprints, calls them a "second sign" (*tekmērion*), and, like a Sherlock Holmes, divides them into two sets, distinguishing "his own and
some companion's." She recognizes them as "like" hers, the heels and
tendons agreeing in their proportions with her own. Yet Electra's conclusion once more points to uncertainty: "On me is anguish and destruc-
tion of mind."

Finally, in the third stage, Orestes appears. In the ensuing dialogue
between brother and sister, Electra continues, even after his revelation
("Here I am"), not to believe him in spite of the signs of the lock of hair
and the footprints. "You are weaving a snare about me," she says. The
burden of proof falls now on Orestes, who plays superbly with Electra's
own previous thoughts: "Flying off, you thought you were beholding me
when you marked the hairlock and the footprints. Now, put to the spot
whence it was shorn the lock of hair and mark how it agrees with that
of my head, and behold this piece of weaving, the work of your own
hands with the hunting scene on it." Electra now accepts him and indeed
bursts into pouring on him the names and love of father, mother, sister,
and brother.

It seems to me that three observations can be made on this complex
scene. In the first place, Aeschylus and his Electra implicitly express a
firm belief in a process which, beginning with the perception of material
clues, examines them rationally and proposes an hypothesis that is
finally validated by "proof." The central mechanism of this process is
constituted by the *syllogismos* Aristotle speaks of in the *Poetics*: somebody like me has come, nobody is like me but Orestes, hence it is

Orestes who has come. However, the progress of this "reasoning" is much more complex and accurate than Aristotle seems to think. Correctly, the first conclusion Electra reaches after examining the lock of hair is that Orestes has *sent* it. Final indication of Orestes' presence can be deduced only from the footprints. What we have here, then, is the first example I know of in Western literature of a *scientific process of deduction* on the stage—a solemn occasion indeed for all of us.

However (and this is the second point), this mechanism is based on certain "signs," and their nature is ambiguous. Lock of hair and footprints cannot by themselves offer conclusive evidence for the hypothesis elaborated by Electra. "Similarity" per se can only produce a hint, a suggestion, but it cannot constitute proof. Similarity in a context (Agamemnon's tomb) goes one step further in furnishing a clue, but it is not final either. Yet the most important thing here is that Aeschylus and Electra are perfectly aware of all this. Electra cries out at the muteness of the signs she has observed, twice in her monologue she says she has a "divided" mind, and even when Orestes reveals himself she refuses to believe him. Once more this moment is significant for the Western mind: it is the moment of doubt. If lock of hair and footprints are "mute" signs which can, however, on the basis of "similarity in context," substantiate an hypothesis, proof is obtained by another "material" sign—the piece of cloth, the work of Electra's own hands, which represents a hunting scene. In passing from lock of hair to footprints, we have already shifted from a "natural," "inherited" sign to an "external" one. Here, the "external" sign (the cloth) is, however, no longer anonymous but bears Electra's own stamp like a signature. It comes from Electra herself, and it has the individual and family mark of a hunt which the entire *Oresteia* uses as a central image of the Atreid house and its destiny. Symbol of civilized man (who weaves and hunts), it is an external sign which contains in its kernel all the strength and significance of inheritance. Electra gave it to Orestes a long time ago, when he had to leave Argos after Agamemnon's murder (the sign prompts us to reconstruct its story and thus go back in time); Orestes gives it back to Electra now. It joins brother and sister, past and present.

And this leads us to the third point, the "artistic" rendering of the scientific process by Aeschylus. Finding of the clues, examination, *syllogismos*, hypothesis, and verification are the outward marks of something deeper, an inner "reasoning" which substantiates them and adds to them an elemental dimension. The rational process is based, as Aristotle quite rightly sees, on a fundamental relationship of "likeness" (this lock of hair and these footprints are like mine). Electra makes it clear in both parts of her speech. This likeness, as I have already remarked, involves not only two individuals (Orestes and Electra) but the species, the family (*us*), as well. Furthermore, as the reasoning progresses toward verification, likeness starts implying identity by its very repetition, until, when accused of weaving a snare against Electra, Orestes replies, "then I devise plots against myself." Orestes is identified as such the moment he identifies with his sister. Electra calls him father, mother, sister, brother.

No wonder Aristotle chose this scene as an example of recognition through reasoning. What must have appealed to him is not only the mechanism but also the clarity and the anguish of the process: the dialogue with oneself, the groping for an answer, the check of reason, the incredibly condensed wordplay, belief, doubt, suspense, surprise, recognition—in short, a beautifully dramatized version of *philosophy* itself. Nor can anyone fail to notice how this initial anagnorisis finds its counterpart in the final one, when Clytemnestra understands that Orestes stands before her, the living incarnation of the snake she has dreamt, sucking her milk and blood, as and because he is killing her: "Stop. Child, respect, son." A servant has just announced Aegisthus's death with the oracular "I say the dead are killing the living ones." In spite of the "enigma," as she herself calls it, Clytemnestra understands. The *Choephoroi* climaxes to a "blood" recognition.

.   .   .

What does Euripides make of anagnorisis in his *Electra?* The recognition between Orestes and his mother toward the end of the play becomes nonimportant. Clytemnestra is killed by both Orestes and Electra, and all we hear of her cries is "O children, in God's name slay not your mother!" But in the first part of the play the question of recognition has been played upon with insistence and suspense. When Orestes arrives in Argos with Pylades, he offers his hair on Agamemnon's tomb and then meets Electra purporting to bring her news of her brother. During their conversation, Electra declares that were Orestes to appear before her, she would be unable to recognize him. "No wonder," replies the stranger, "you were both young when you were parted." Electra concludes that only the old man who had been Agamemnon's tutor would be able to recognize her brother. She does not notice that her interlocutor seems to know a lot about their story, for he interrupts her with, "The man who, they say, stole him away from murder?"

Euripides, in other words, thematically prepares the ground for the recognition while laying it waste intellectually. Anagnorisis is impossible unless through a witness. Accordingly, Euripides splits the recognition scene proper into two halves in the first of which he attacks Aeschylus's solution, while in the second he offers his own. The burden of representing Aeschylus's position and being teased for it falls on the old man, who, upon meeting Electra, tells her that he has seen a lock of hair on Agamemnon's grave. Perhaps, he says, Orestes has come in secret to visit the place. No other Argive would. "Go there yourself," he concludes, "and put that hair against your own. See if their colour tallies. Children of one father often have many features that are similar." Now, we know that Orestes has indeed left his hair on Agamemnon's tomb, and thus the old man's inference is correct. But Electra destroys his argument by attacking the specific validity of the clue, of the "similarity" syllogism, and of its context. As to the latter, a brave man like Orestes would not come secretly, as if he feared Aegisthus. Then, how could the two locks correspond if one belongs to a noble young man trained in the palaestra while the other is a woman's and softened with combing? It is "impossible." Finally, one would find many people with hair of a similar colour even if they are not of the same blood.

Having thus disposed of Aeschylus's first clue, Euripides proceeds to attack the second. The old man invites Electra to go and try the footprint: "see if it is *symmetros* to your foot." Aeschylus's Electra had maintained that the heels and markings of the footprints, if *metroumenai*, would coincide perfectly with her own, while she had used *symmetros* for the lock of hair. The point would be crucial in a detective enquiry, for *metros*, the root of both words, expresses "measure" in the typically Greek sense of "proportion." Hence, the Aeschylean Electra seems to be saying that the footprints have the same general outlook as hers and that in their proportion they coincide with hers. When he uses *symmetros*, Euripides' old man keeps Aeschylus's ambiguity, though he emphasizes the likeness (*sym*). But when Electra fires her reply the ambiguity has disappeared. Again, she criticizes the context first: "how could there be footprints on rocky ground?" Then, she eliminates the *metros* (proportioned) replacing it with *isos* (equal): "And if there could be footprints, brother's and sister's feet would not be the *same size*. A man has bigger feet."

Not satisfied with having destroyed the clues, Euripides attempts an attack on Aeschylus's concluding evidence, too. When the old man asks Electra, "If your brother were here, would there not be to recognize him the cloak, woven on your loom and with which I stole him away from death?" she replies that when Orestes left, she was a child (which means that she could not have been weaving anything) and besides he would not be wearing now the same cloak he had in infancy, because clothes do not grow larger with the body. This attack rests mainly on context. The error Aeschylus has made, Euripides says, is serious—not just one that depends on ambiguous signs and faulty reasoning but a mistake in dramatic verisimilitude. When Orestes left, Electra was a child.

Aeschylus's whole recognition mechanism is thus exposed. Euripides leaves the solution for the second half of his scene, when Orestes appears onstage. The old man, as Orestes himself remarks, stares at him "as if examining the shining image on the silver" and paces around him. After some hesitation, he recognizes the young man by a scar on his brow, which Orestes cut when as a child he fell while chasing a fawn with Electra. By introducing this last factual detail, Euripides avoids a possible accusation of paralogism ("not everyone who has a scar on his brow is Orestes"). Electra, "convinced by all the signs" (*symboloisi*) of the old man, embraces her brother.

The introduction of a third person into the episode makes a difference. Euripides stages the scene between Electra and the old man as if it were a discussion such as those that Protagoras, Gorgias, or indeed Socrates could have held—a dialogue, a logical debate on a specific question: how can you prove a man's identity? Attached and functional to this is the parody and hence the critical discussion of Aeschylus's anagnorisis process. Euripides does not deny the validity of the process as such, the reasoning of Aeschylus's Electra. He attacks the specific value of Aeschylus's signs and the context in which they are inserted. His Electra is a sharp sophist. As Aristophanes ironically makes Euripides say of himself in the *Frogs*,

I taught them all these knowing ways
By chopping logic in my plays,
And making all my speakers try
To reason out the How and the Why.

Euripides does make Orestes leave the lock of hair on Agamemnon's tomb, but he maintains that as a sign this is not sufficient to constitute the basis for a *syllogismos*. He proclaims that in this particular instance, in this context, only an eyewitness can prove Orestes' identity. When the old man finds the "acquired sign on the body"—the scar on the brow—which he can tie to a particular episode in Orestes' life, and after he has attentively scrutinized the young man, then *all* the signs start meaning something and Electra is convinced. Euripides' treatment of Aeschylus's scene marks a new development in the history of Western "reasoning"— one that strikes a note of caution against the use of rationality and scientific processes. In doing this, Euripides brings to their extreme logical consequence the doubt and the anguish at the muteness of signs of Aeschylus's Electra. He invites us to look at the particulars, and nobody after him has been able to reproduce Aeschylus's *syllogismos* until modern science offered the quantitative and qualitative means to assess the probatory value of signs: until, that is, Electra's clues are replaced by forensic evidence. Euripides' position is, moreover, particularly delicate, in that he accepts the tradition according to which Orestes consecrates his hair on Agamemnon's tomb, thus making the audience aware that one of the signs Electra so logically refutes is indeed a truthful one—a contradiction which will be amplified by Sophocles with his "trick" of the urn. Conditioned by so many factors, no wonder that Euripides' final answer should be less intellectually intense than Aeschylus's. Instead of relying for its effect on the mounting anguish of reason, on the excitement of a new tool brought to bear on human affairs, it becomes an intellectual game which resorts to surprise and tradition at the same time. After the critique of Aeschylus's clues—which of course destroys the *Choephoroi*'s use of "inner reasoning" as well—we are left with no ground. The old man's attentive perusal of Orestes comes unexpected, and we all share Electra's and Orestes' "wonder" as it raises to a climax with the observer's cryptic revelation, "My daughter, royal Electra! Pray to the great gods." When Electra asks him, "For what, for things that are not or for things that are?" he replies with a significant remark: "To grasp the precious treasure that God reveals." Orestes' identification is like a divine revelation, a materialization at which the audience feels total surprise because it comes after a long logical exchange which has proved that Orestes cannot be present. The scar, too, about which we knew nothing before, is surprising. Nothing, after all, can be more unexpected in this intellectual atmosphere than finding a Homeric solution to the ever present problem of recognition—Odysseus's scar beheld by a male nurse.

.   .   .

We have already seen how Sophocles turns recognition into a central plot of his *Electra* and what this does to the overall meaning of the play. The question we must ask now is how he deals with the problems raised by Aeschylus's and Euripides' two contrasting versions of the recognition scene. In Sophocles, this takes place after two subplots and two false recognitions within them. In the first place, Chrysotemis reports to Electra Clytemnestra's dream. The Chorus's description of this dream in the *Choephoroi* comes out at a much later stage, thus confirming Orestes' resolution to kill his mother. In Sophocles' *Electra*, on the other hand, the dream foreshadows Orestes' return and revenge. Its content has changed: instead of linking Orestes to his mother, it ties father and son. Agamemnon has appeared, taken the sceptre and planted it by the household altar. From it springs and spreads a fruitful bough, until it overshadows all Mycenae's land. No explanation is given, but it is clear that the dream anticipates some future event. Our expectation is titillated.

Second, after the old man's announcement of Orestes' death, Chrysotemis reveals to Electra that their brother is alive and near. She declares she has herself seen "certain signs" (*saphē sēmeia*) of it, and when Electra asks her what "proof" (*pistis*) she has, Chrysotemis tells her story. As she reached the old tomb of their father, she saw milk recently poured flow down from it and the grave itself surrounded by flowers. Wonder seized her. She turned around to see if anyone was coming, but the place was deserted and she cautiously approached the tomb. There, she saw a lock of hair:

> And as soon as I saw it, a familiar light burst into my soul, that I was seeing a sign (*tekmerion*) of Orestes, the dearest of all men to me. I took the lock into my hands without saying a word in order not to

spoil that omen of happiness, and tears sprang to my eyes. And even now I am certain that that offering can come only from him. Who can bring there an offering but you and me? I know that I have not done so, nor you. And how? You are not allowed to leave the house, even to pray the gods, without being punished. Neither are our mother's thoughts accustomed to busy themselves with such things, nor could she have done it without being seen. Those offerings are Orestes'.

This passage full of emotion is Sophocles' first answer to the Aeschylus-Euripides dilemma. Sophocles, too, uses the lock of hair and makes Chrysotemis consider it a sign or a proof, but instead of having her rationally infer that it is Orestes' because it is similar to hers, he swiftly dips into the mystery of association and memory. A sudden "luminous form" invades Chrysotemis's soul—the image-thought of seeing a sign of Orestes. For the moment, there is no hint of rationality at work. Chrysotemis picks up the lock of hair as if to appropriate the sign, to touch with her hands the evidence of her own feeling and thinking, and, surrounded by silence, bursts into tears. For her, recognition is effected.

The *syllogismos* belongs to the present; it is a later rationalization of a past intuitive process. Now, one can reason by exclusion: if it is neither me nor you nor our mother, then it must be Orestes. After Euripides' critique, Sophocles eliminates the concept of similarity which was the basic mechanism of Aeschylus's *syllogismos* but sticks to reasoning, implicitly declaring it possible and indeed in a human mind directly consequent upon the apprehension of reality by means of an intuition dominated by emotion. At the same time, Sophocles slowly transforms Chrysotemis's evaluation of the "sign" she meets. At first, this is only a potential *tekmerion,* a sign supposed to be a sign, but when Chrysotemis tells the story to Electra, it has become a set of signs endowed with certainty.

Finally, another trick is played before our eyes. The material sign, eloquent to Chrysotemis's intuition, is shown to be twice as mute here as in Aeschylus when the voice of a witness overwhelms it. Electra replies to Chrysotemis's report, "You know not whither on earth or whither in your mind you are carried," and when her sister retorts with the certainty that firsthand, ocular knowledge gives her ("How could I not know what I saw clearly?"), she reveals that Orestes is dead and this has been announced by a man who witnessed the event. Hence the offerings found on Agamemnon's tomb must be an anonymous homage to Orestes' memory. Recognition is proved to be *méconnaissance* while we know its knowledge to be truthful. As after Clytemnestra's dream our expectation had risen to a climax with Chrysotemis's report, so now it falls back into uncertainty. We know that Orestes is alive and here. But how is our knowledge to become the play's anagnorisis if Orestes is, to all effects, dead for the characters—if the lock of hair is replaced by the urn?

When this, the apparently final testimony of a life now ended, is recognized by Electra as the truthful sign (*emphanē tekmēria*) in spite of its total muteness, the audience knows that Sophocles is staging a misrecognition and expects this inextricable knot of reality, appearance, knowledge, and ignorance to be untied. In fact, the dénouement takes place in the very same scene, and it contains a double recognition. The urn, accompanied by Orestes, appears before Electra. She is allowed to take it in her hand and pronounces a moving lament on it. As her last words mingle with the Chorus's philosophical consolation, Orestes feels he cannot keep up his pretence and recognizes his sister: "Alas, alas! What shall I say? Whither, at a loss for words, shall I go? I have no more strength to dominate my tongue. Is this form of yours the noble form of Electra?" The dialogue between the two unfolds quickly now. When Electra remarks that her interlocutor is the only one to show compassion toward her, he replies, "The only one, in fact, who approaches you suffering your very same woes." Electra at once thinks he might be a distant relative. Orestes decides to tell her everything. The urn contains Orestes' ashes only because a tale has made it look like it. The grave of that unhappy man does not exist, because the living have no tomb. And the riddle precipitates truth and recognition.

ELECTRA: What do you mean, my child?
ORESTES: There is nothing untrue in my words.
ELECTRA: Is he then a living man?
ORESTES: Yes, if breath is in me.
ELECTRA: Are you then he?
ORESTES: Examine this, my father's ring and see if
         I speak the truth.
ELECTRA: O beloved light!
ORESTES: Beloved, I am its witness.
ELECTRA: O voice—are you there?

ORESTES: No longer question elsewhere.
ELECTRA: I have you in my arms?
ORESTES: Thus henceforth forever hold me.
ELECTRA: O dearest women, fellow-citizens, you see
in this man, Orestes, dead by devising
now by devising saved.

For the finale of his scene, Sophocles resorts to Aeschylus's technique: it is words that unveil Orestes' identity, it is a ring—but the ring of the "House," of Agamemnon—that proves it. Dream, lock of hair, urn, are finally replaced by a true sign which substantiates, and at the same time is substantiated by, the presence of a living man. With the "voice," out come truth and light and recognition of the devices, the *mekhanai* of death and life. Anagnorisis is revelation—and in such a setting that it has allowed Simon Weil to see it as a "pre-Christian intuition" of the mutual recognition of God and man, as a scene which resembles that between Mary Magdalene and a "certain gardener."

Be that as it may, it seems clear to me that the eighty-year-old Sophocles who composed the *Electra* chose a recognition mechanism which goes beyond both the empassioned rationalism of Aeschylus and the wonder-seeking intellectualism of Euripides while taking both into account. The man who, as we shall see in the last chapter of this volume, had built up the inexorable concatenation of events and deductions in Oedipus's detective enquiry, knew the value of signs and of reason as well as the importance of *méconnaissance*. In *Electra,* he continued his exploration. His solution was not to indict signs by means of "reasoning" but to show how they can be right or wrong depending on the reality we assume to be true, to point out how "devices" can create both death and life. By multiplying characters, plots, and signs, by immersing them in a mixed light of emotion, rationality, and enigma, he made the theme and scene of anagnorisis the problematic pivots of his *Electra.* It is by no means insignificant that when, in yet another recognition episode, an increasingly mad Electra recognizes the old man as her "father" and "saviour," he should cut her short with a sentence which delays full knowledge to an indefinite future of tale-telling: "As for the words that stand in between, / many nights revolve and matching days / which will reveal these things to you / clearly, Electra."

If, then, all three tragedians agree that ultimate proof of Orestes' return and identity must be an "acquired" sign, there is no doubt that the process by which they lead us to it is very different. The way in which they deal with this famous recognition scene depends of course on their temperament and their approach to dramatic art. But it also clearly shows different attitudes to a problem which is ultimately philosophical—what is anagnorisis, the shift from ignorance to knowledge?—and within it to a basically epistemological question: what is the value of signs, clues, reasoning? To these questions Aeschylus, Euripides, and Sophocles offer the different answers I have tried to indicate. With his burning satire of Aeschylus, Euripides wants to revolutionize the model but ultimately resorts to tradition. Sophocles is happy with "improving" the invention with a series of extraordinary theatrical and psychological inventions. However, the dilemma of Orestes' and Electra's recognition stands there for us as a paradigm of the problem of knowledge which, as Aristotle might have put it, both poetry and philosophy face. The intense debate on this scene that dramatists and philosophers pursue between the fifth and fourth centuries B.C.E. seems to be a witness to this as well as to the coming to awareness—the self-recognition—of Greek culture. The question to which I now turn is what modern treatments of the Electra-Orestes recognition scene can tell us about our culture.

·   ·   ·

A first answer may be provided by Robert Lowell's translation for the stage of Aeschylus's *Oresteia* as recently as 1977. Here, Orestes offers on Agamemnon's tomb "these locks of my hair, this blood-knot / of red feathers dipped in blood," which Electra and the Chorus find as they pour libations on the grave. Interestingly, however, only fragments of Aeschylus's "reasoning" are left, and they are themselves inserted into a different context. When Lowell's Electra sees the blood-knot "tied with human hair," she immediately concludes that "they couldn't have come from our house," and, asked by the Chorus who could have brought them, she replies, "Someone who has sworn to avenge Agamemnon—I think Orestes may have *sent* them." The Chorus retorts that Orestes would not dare *return* to Argos. The *syllogismos* has changed. There is no question of similarity here but only one of context. As Electra puts it, "whoever left it [the knot of eagle feathers] wished to avenge my Father's

murder. I think Orestes . . . " She herself leaves the conclusion totally tentative: "The gods know." Significantly, what is left of Aeschylus's scene
is Electra's anguish, her doubt, her cry at the muteness of signs: "I wish
these feathers had a voice . . . Oh this confusion! My mind is groping."
On the other hand, Lowell's Electra reacts to the sight of the "eagle-
feathers" somewhat like Sophocles' Chrysotemis when she finds the lock
of hair: "But when I look at these / red feathers, it's as though someone /
has slashed a sword across my heart. / It's as though my own blood had
stained them."

Aeschylus's "external" sign becomes "internal." Instead of—however
mute—objects, we have an entirely subjective feeling, which transforms
the "reasoning by similarity" into a sudden deep flash of total identity.
Electra no longer says, "This hair is like ours, like mine," but "it's *as
though my own blood stained them.*" Lowell keeps a hint of the Sophoclean
Chrysotemis's reasoning by exclusion: for a second, his Electra thinks
that her mother, or rather "the mistress of Aegisthus," "left this knot of
eagle feathers to tell [her] [she] must die." The American poet has also
eliminated the footprints and changed the first "sign" itself, making his
more Aeschylean than Aeschylus himself had ever imagined it. Orestes'
hair is marginal in Lowell's scene. What counts here is the knot of eagle
feathers dipped in blood, the eagle being the very symbol of the Atreid
house as consecrated in the *Oresteia.* Similarly, final proof of Orestes'
identity is no longer just a cloth with a hunting scene woven by Electra
but a piece of *tapestry* embroidered by her and sent to Orestes in his exile
(which disposes of Euripides' double criticism, of the vestment and of
the incongruity of Electra weaving anything as a child). It represents not
just *a* hunting scene connected with the general imagery of the *Oresteia*
but a hunter killing a wolf and his bitch—a clear allusion to Orestes'
murder of Aegisthus and Clytemnestra.

In this terse modern version, then, the powerful mechanism of Aeschylus's deduction and doubt has disappeared, and the clues on which
it was based have significantly changed. Lowell's Electra seems to give
up the possibility of knowledge: "The gods know. We pray to the gods,—
and they spin us round in circles like sailors." All this happens in what
purports to be a translation of Aeschylus's *Oresteia,* and that Lowell has
felt the need to interpret and adapt the recognition mechanism of his
original for a twentieth-century stage should make us pause.

Obviously, a modern author cannot turn Electra into a 100 percent Sherlock Holmes or transform her clues into forensic evidence without turning the *Choephoroi* itself into a comedy. Our scientific, archaeological mentality would not accept such a massive intrusion of twentieth-century assumptions and criteria into classical myth. Yet if Robert Lowell feels free to change Aeschylus's signs and conclusive evidence, clues could be found from which to deduce Orestes' presence with a higher degree of certainty—for instance, a sequel of eagle's feathers and a piece of writing. As soon as we envisage this kind of solution, however, we realize that in fact it would destroy the recognition scene. If Electra obtained conclusive evidence of Orestes' return before he actually appears to her, the anagnorisis would become a purely mechanical question of exhibiting and recognizing a token—a ring, a scar, eventually an identity card or a DNA test—as indeed is the case in many operas, detective novels, films, and modern police enquiries. In other words, we realize that dramatic recognition "through reasoning" cannot do without the thrill of scenic ambiguity and rational uncertainty, for to stage the process of knowledge by means of reasoning a play must give us the same excitement and anguish that finding the clues, inferring, doubting, and obtaining proof make us feel in scientific or philosophical research.

Is there a solution, then, to the problem of the Orestes-Electra recognition for a modern artist—one, that is, who knows classical treatments of the scene, cannot accept Aeschylus's version after Euripides' critique, but cannot change its mechanism radically for reasons which are at once philological, artistic, and epistemological? There are, I would say, three kinds of solutions. The first is to eliminate "reason" altogether. The second consists in making the recognition itself insignificant. The third resorts to a complex procedure, which explores the dilemma itself without resolving it.

To examine these three solutions in detail would far exceed the limits of the present chapter. But even a rapid survey of modern versions of the *sujet* of *Electra* will show interesting changes in the role of reason in recognition. It is certainly remarkable that two dramatists of the Age of Reason should opt for the first solution, which leaves reason and signs no decisive part to play in the recognition proper. In Voltaire's *Oreste* (first staged in 1750) Electra accepts Orestes' identity ultimately in an act of faith invoking the force of "nature" and the "voice of blood":

Yes, I love him; yea methinks
I see my father's features, I hear his voice;
Nature speaks to us and pierces this mystery.
Do not make resistance to her: yea, you are my brother.
You are. I see you. I embrace you.

While in Voltaire's play signs are still allowed a certain, though secondary and noncrucial, part, in Alfieri's *Oreste* (first performed in 1781) they
are totally eliminated. The anagnorisis scene in Act II, scene ii, is preceded by no signs, or any *syllogismos*. Electra recognizes her brother only
"al tuo furor" (for your fury) and asks him to recognize her "al duolo, al
pianto, all'amor mio" (because of her woe, weeping, and love). Reason is
replaced by feelings; the signs are now Orestes' uncontrolled fury and
wish for revenge and Electra's tears. It is in fact by forgetting himself, by
abandoning prudence and reason, that Orestes reveals himself.

Alfieri's recognition scene, so typical of his temperament and his
style, is emblematic of a poet who, nourished by the culture of the
Enlightenment, reacted against it to the point of being considered a
"proto-romantic." A century and a half later, when in 1903–4 Hugo von
Hofmannsthal wrote, after Sophocles, his one-act play *Elektra* (for which
Richard Strauss provided a memorable score), the cultural situation had
profoundly changed, but the solution to the recognition problem of Electra and Orestes remained basically the same.

In this drama (and opera) the anagnorisis is, as in Sophocles, double: Electra and Orestes have to recognize each other, but the plots and
counterplots leading to recognition in classical tragedy have disappeared.
Chrysotemis finds no lock of hair on Agamemnon's tomb, no urn is carried on the stage, and there is no final recognition between Orestes on
the one hand and Clytemnestra and Aegisthus on the other. What is left
of the Sophoclean mythos is the announcement of Orestes' death; and
what is added to it is the theme of Electra's obsessive waiting for her
brother, which pervades the earlier part of the play. Thus, the crucial
anagnorisis between Orestes and Electra constitutes the real climax of
the piece—as Strauss's music makes clear and as Ernst Bloch underlined
almost thirty years ago.

Orestes, having recognized Electra by her grief over his pretended
death, is in turn recognized by her only after a dog has greeted him and
an old servant has kissed his feet. Recognition has changed its purpose

as well as its mechanisms. In recognizing Orestes, Electra's mind, devoted to a revenge which no longer bears any trace of justice, breaks up and runs at once toward darkness, madness, and nothingness. Anagnorisis is a passage from ignorance to an even greater ignorance. The clues, the reasoning, the proofs of Aeschylus are gone. The opposed signs, the memory, the flashes, the ambiguity of Sophocles have disappeared. What replaces them is the significant question, hammered out throughout the scene, "Wer bist du?" "Who are you?" It is words and the way they are pronounced, signifying a whole universe of hidden feelings and reality, that produce the recognition. Superimposed upon mute gestures, it is Orestes' intonation that convinces Electra. The old servant kisses his feet in silence and the master addresses his sister:

> Die Hunde auf dem Hof erkennen mich,
> und meine Schwester nicht?
> (The dogs of the house recognize me,
> and my sister does not?)

Hofmannsthal has turned Orestes into Odysseus and fused with a masterly stroke the dog Argos and the nurse Eurycleia into a single line and a silent kiss. He shows us the way a genius can improve the invention of Sophocles by means of another's invention: Homer's.

If Alfieri's and Hofmannsthal's are indicative of the first solution a modern artist can give to the problem of the Orestes-Electra recognition, that of eliminating "reason" altogether, the second possibility—rendering recognition meaningless—can be observed in two other modern plays. In O'Neill's *Mourning Becomes Electra* (1932), Electra becomes Lavinia and Orestes is Orin. They are the offspring of a New England family in the 1860s, the Mannons. Their father, General Ezra Mannon, returns home after the Civil War and is poisoned by Captain Brant at the instigation of Mannon's wife, Christine, who has a relationship with him. When Orin, too, comes back from the war, he and Lavinia avenge their father's murder. It becomes increasingly clear that O'Neill makes overt use of Freud's Oedipus and Electra complexes: Orin hates his father and loves his mother, while Lavinia adores the former and despises the latter. But the point to notice from our angle is that in this setting the Electra-Orestes recognition becomes completely unnecessary, and in fact O'Neill eliminates it altogether.

Five years later, in 1937, the French author, Jean Giraudoux, produced an *Electre* in which the protagonist only suspects that her father has been murdered and receives confirmation of this in a dream, while Argos lives an undisturbed life of peace ruled by Clytemnestra and her lover Aegisthus. Here, Orestes appears as a "stranger" who reveals himself to Electra by simply pronouncing his name. Likewise, Clytemnestra understands but a little later (long before being killed) and without any particular excitement that the stranger is her son. In this totally unheroic atmosphere, recognition loses its importance: it becomes an ordinary event which requires no special mechanism and prompts but a passing emotion. "Tu es Oreste!" exclaims Electra when the stranger declares that his name is that which alone, as she says, can draw her toward a human being. Orestes simply replies, "O ungrateful sister, who recognize me by my name only!" Then, the scene ends abruptly with Clytemnestra appearing onstage.

At first glance, the recognition between Electra and Orestes in Jean-Paul Sartre's *Les Mouches* (The Flies, 1943) looks similarly uncomplicated. Orestes, previously introduced as Philebe, makes himself known to his sister by saying, "Electre, je suis Oreste." We soon realize, however, that in this play anagnorisis becomes an important theme. The recognition scene itself is split into three stages. Initially, Orestes recognizes Electra because she reveals her own name. Then, when in his turn he says who he is, she refuses to accept him as Orestes because he does not correspond to her image of him and is unwilling to act and think as she wishes. Finally, when he changes his mind, she calls him "Orestes!"

In this context, recognition becomes a philosophical motif, sounded from the very beginning of the play. In the first scene the pedagogue remarks to Orestes that the flies seem to recognize him. One second later, Jupiter introduces himself as Demetrios, and the play on his identity will continue until the second scene of the third act. In *The Flies*, recognition is the acquisition of consciousness and decidedness. Orestes is recognized as such by Electra when he realizes that he must "descend" toward others, say farewell to his "lightness," become a "voleur de remords." The flies, which "seem" to recognize him at the beginning, stick to him—and to him alone—at the end.

Parallel to this process of recognition by which Orestes starts incarnating his mythological self by becoming a true human being, another takes place which brings him to recognize Demetrios as Jupiter. Here,

Sartre plays on the traditional theme of theophany, recognition and mis-recognition of gods. At the end of the play, Jupiter acts the part of the Creator, of the supreme ruler of an harmonious universe in which Orestes is only a "mite" who has committed evil. But Orestes replies: "You are the king of the Gods, Jupiter, the king of stones and stars, the king of the waves of the sea. But you are not the king of men." Recognition between human beings has little value, too. When, after the murder of Aegisthus, Electra, now full of horror, tells her brother there is no need to kill Clytemnestra as well, Orestes says he "recognizes" her no longer, and she replies: "je ne te reconnais non plus." The ancient story of anagnorisis between Electra and Orestes is finished forever. In Marguerite Yource-nar's *Electre* (1954), the scene has in fact disappeared.

Far from making recognition insignificant, Sartre turns it into an existential problem. In doing so, however, he stresses its insolubility. Not only does he eliminate reason from the Electra-Orestes anagnorisis, but he makes recognition dependent upon one person's acceptance of another's image of him. When this coincidence of images and purposes ends, when two consciousnesses start conflicting, anagnorisis is denied. People—or gods—continue to exist, but they cannot be known anymore.

Post-Aeschylean treatments of the Orestes-Electra scene prove, then, that it contains a dilemma which the Western mind, or at least Western literature, seems incapable of solving—a dilemma centred upon the value of signs and "reasoning" and ultimately of "cognition" itself. Can one find counterproof of this in a work of literature that does not make use of Electra and Orestes? The answer to this question cannot but be affirmative if one thinks of the paradigmatic postclassical tragedy of the West, Shakespeare's *Hamlet*.

·   ·   ·

In Pirandello's *Il fu Mattia Pascal* (The Late Mattia Pascal, 1904) a friend tells the protagonist that a puppet theatre is going to stage the tragedy of Orestes "d'après Sophocle" and invites him to imagine the culminat-ing moment of it, "when the puppet representing Orestes is about to revenge his father's death on his mother and Aegisthus." At that point, the paper sky of the puppet theatre would suddenly be rent. What would happen then? "Orestes would be terribly disconcerted by that hole in the sky. He would still feel the urge towards revenge, but his eyes would go to the tear and his arms would fall." Destroy the veil of faith in the

supernatural, endow an ancient hero with self-reflecting conscience—
Pirandello seems to be saying—and you have the protagonist of modern
tragedy. "*Orestes would become Hamlet.*" In fact, affinities between the stories of Orestes and Hamlet were first detected, if we are to believe Henry
James Pye, in the eighteenth century, when the French abbot Prevot
wrote "a comparison between the tragedies of Electra and Hamlet, in
which 'he commends the English poet because wiser than Sophocles, he
forbids young Hamlet, by the apparition of the ghost, to attempt anything against his mother's life.'" Pye's quotation and short discussion of
this comparison occur in his second note to chapter 14 of the *Poetics*—
the chapter, that is, in which Aristotle discusses the various combinations
of action, inaction, ignorance, knowledge, and anagnorisis in a tragedy.
For Aristotle, the worst possible way of arranging these elements in order
to produce pity or fear consists in having a character "know and intend
to act and then refrain from acting." This, he says, "has a morally repul-
sive quality and is not tragic, because there is no disaster." In his *Second
Discours sur la Tragédie* (1660), Corneille, fearful that Aristotle's con-
demnation, if not corrected, might include his own *Cid, Cinna,* and other
works, limits its purport by saying that "it must be intended only of those
who know the person they want to ruin and draw back by a simple
change of will, without being forced by a notable event and without any
loss of power on their part."

Whether we agree with Aristotle or Corneille, in a general fashion
both their statements seem to fit Hamlet's plight extremely well, for Hamlet "knows" his uncle Claudius and his mother Gertrude and intends
to kill the former, but he refrains from doing so until the very end of
the play. Yet as soon as we say this, we realize that something is missing
from our picture, namely, a clear idea of Hamlet's "knowledge" and of his
knowledge of Claudius and Gertrude in particular.

What Hamlet knows as the play begins is that his mother has married her husband's brother a month after the former's death—that she
has posted "with such dexterity to incestuous sheets." He knows this "is
not, nor it cannot come to good," and he knows his own state of mind
about it. Significantly, he voices his feelings before harping on the particular "fact" which at this point appears to us as their main cause. His
first great monologue in the play opens with one of those general, intro-
spective, melancholy series of reflections which have made him dear to

all audiences. He wishes "that this too too sullied flesh would melt, / Thaw and resolve itself into a dew, / Or that the Everlasting had not fix'd / His canon 'gainst self slaughter." He feels "all the uses of this world" to be—to him—"weary, stale, flat and unprofitable," the world itself "an unweeded garden/That grows to seed," "things rank and gross in nature" possessing it entirely.

Such is Hamlet's knowledge, an inner awareness of what *is* inside him ("I know not 'seems' / . . . I have that within that passes show") and of how the world without is reflected, "seems" in him ("seem to me all the uses of the world!"), as opposed to the purely external and obviously true knowledge Gertrude would have him assent to:

> Thou know'st 'tis common. All that lives must die,
> Passing through nature to eternity.

Hamlet, and we with him, gains more factual knowledge about Claudius and Gertrude from the Ghost. Scenes i and iv of Act I are the great recognition scenes of *Hamlet*—which, contrary to all the plays we have so far studied, thus begins with anagnorisis. Scene v contains the "revelation": in it, the Ghost unfolds the truth about his death, the murder of King Hamlet by his brother Claudius. The second section of scene ii links the first and second recognition scenes and prepares the revelation.

With Barnardo's "Who's there?"—the first words of the play—the first scene of *Hamlet* plunges us into the atmosphere of uncertain expectation and mystery that Coleridge so much praised. It is a "bitter cold" midnight, and the sentry on guard, Francisco, whom Barnardo comes to relieve, is, for unknown reasons, "sick at heart." The night has so far been quiet, perhaps too quiet—"not a mouse stirring." But when Horatio emerges out of the darkness, the battlement of the castle is suddenly filled by words indicating a mysterious presence: "What, has this thing appear'd again tonight?" The sceptical Horatio will call "this thing" the others' "fantasy" "and will not let belief take hold of him." Against his ironical detachment stands Barnardo's and Marcellus's fear, based on what they have twice witnessed, that the "dreaded sight" might appear again. And as soon as Barnardo starts recounting what happened the night before, "it comes again" "in the same figure like the King that's dead." Horatio, the scholar now harrowed "with fear and wonder," must discover the identity and the business of the Ghost. Both he and his friends, however, refrain from accepting "him" as in fact the dead king. They insist on "its" mere, though perfect, "likeness" to Hamlet's father while proving its objective reality through "the sensible and true avouch / of [their] own eyes"—that is, the evidence of their senses.

We have here the most uncanny anagnorisis so far encountered. There is no doubt that "this thing" is now recognized as "something more than fantasy"—as, indeed, a "thing"—and that it looks "like" the dead king. Its nature, however, is totally mysterious, as Horatio makes explicit by asking it,

> What art thou that usurp'st this time of night,
> Together with that fair and warlike form
> In which the majesty of buried Denmark
> Did sometimes march?

Horatio's and his friends' enquiry is as perceptive and rational as the Aeschylean Electra's. They remark that the "apparition" is as "like" the king as Barnardo is "to himself," that "Such was the very armour he had on / When he th'ambitious Norway combated," and that "So frown'd he once." They explore the causes that may have produced the appearance of "this portentous figure." When Horatio recounts that Norway and Denmark had a feud which is being renewed by the young Norwegian Fortinbras in an attempt to recover the land lost by his father to King Hamlet, Barnardo at once seizes on this situation as the possible explanation of the Ghost's coming. Horatio, who significantly proclaims this inference a "mote to trouble the mind's eye," yet adds as an historical parallel the events—including the squeaking and gibbering of the "sheeted dead" in the streets—which took place in Rome "a little ere the mightiest Julius fell." The Ghost, in other words, is considered an omen, a "sign." Like Electra with the lock of hair, Horatio wishes it had a voice and indeed six times charges it to speak. When the Ghost reappears, Horatio addresses it with a fourfold conjuration which also contains three hypotheses to explain its coming. Something "good" might be done to ease its condition. Or the Ghost may know things regarding the country's fate which could be avoided if disclosed. Finally, the Ghost might reveal the existence of a hidden treasure.

All this reasoning comes to naught. The cock crows, and although the Ghost apparently is about to speak and the three friends try to stop it from going, it disappears. Horatio's conclusion is that the Ghost seems "like a guilty thing" for which the cock's crowing represents "a fearful summons." Indeed, the "present object" makes "probation" of the "truth" of the proposition according to which the cock awakes with his crowing the "god of day . . . , and at his warning, / Whether in sea or fire, in earth or air, / Th'extravagant and erring spirit hies to his confine." Horatio now knows that this "fantasy," this "illusion" is a "spirit."

As a recognition scene, this passage is not only unfulfilling but in fact alienating. The knowledge Horatio, Barnardo, and Marcellus gain is purely visual: naked sense perception. The various *syllogismoi* they elaborate apprehend only a partial "what," never a "how" or a "why." The "ghostliness" of the Ghost and its likeness to the dead king are blank facts, whose real nature and causes remain obscure and problematical— "a mote to trouble the mind's eye." The "object" of this knowledge is a "thing"; it may be a "guilty thing," it may be a "sign." The truth is, it is elusive, "invulnerable" "as the air," "dumb." The effect on the spectator of this state of affairs is that her or his disbelief cannot be suspended any longer yet is only half removed. While the action sets us in expectation of recognition, words and silences plunge us into a deeper level, where the certainty of knowledge is radically, irremediably questioned. It is a situation which symbolically enacts the continuous tension that characterises the gnoseological status of *Hamlet*.

When, in the second half of scene ii Hamlet, having vented his spleen and discussed the inner awareness he has of external facts, is informed by Horatio of the night's events, he, too, must face this problem. The exchange which introduces Horatio's disclosure is significant. "My father," the prince says, and, after a pause, "methinks I see my father." Horatio's inevitable question, "Where, my lord?" at once sends us back to the atmosphere of tension and uncanniness of the first scene. Hamlet's reply, "In my mind's eye, Horatio," is a resolution in appearance only. It signals the fact that Hamlet's thoughts circle continuously around the image of his father, his death, his mother's hasty new marriage, but it also announces a fundamental problem of the play, the suggestion that Hamlet's vision of his father's Ghost may be, as Gertrude will tell him later, "the very coinage of [his] brain." For the moment, Hamlet's phrase heightens the suspense, while Horatio's rejoinder alleviates it by going back to past reality and building up the image of the dead king—an ideal monarch and, as Hamlet adds, a true man: "I saw him once; a was a goodly king"; "a was a man, take him for all in all." The objective reality of "seeing" and "being" in the past is, however, suddenly replaced by the disquieting impression of a present vision. "My lord," Horatio says, "I think I saw him yesternight." Quite naturally, Hamlet replies in amazement, "Saw? Who?"

Horatio's account of the Ghost's apparition first to Barnardo and Marcellus and then to himself progressively underlines its "likeness" to the king. The "figure like your father" of his first words becomes, in his last, so similar to King Hamlet as Horatio's hands are to each other: "I knew your father; / These hands are not more like." Interestingly enough, Horatio does not make clear whether his "knowing" is past knowledge of the king or present recognition of him in the Ghost's figure. By using the image of the two hands to indicate the likeness, he does not go beyond the mirrorlike individuality of two separate objects. Quite understandably Hamlet, though startled by this account, is not satisfied with it and begins a truly policelike interrogation. "Where was this?" "Did you not speak to it?" he starts but soon turns to the crucial problem of establishing the exact nature of the "likeness" proclaimed by his friend. In both questions and answers, the Ghost is referred to as sometimes a thing ("it") and sometimes a person ("he"). Hamlet learns the following facts: the Ghost was armed from top to toe, but "his" face was visible as "he wore his beaver up"; his countenance was sorrowful and "very pale" rather than angry; he fixed his eyes constantly on Horatio; "it" "stay'd" "while one with moderate haste might tell a hundred"; and finally, his beard was "grizzled" or, as Horatio specifies, "a sable silver'd" as it was "in his life." Here, we have a scientific enquiry turning upon the basic coordinates of the phenomenon: place, duration, appearance, movements. But one cannot examine with the tools of reason the data of a phenomenon which Horatio himself calls a "marvel." One can only accept its factuality as witnessed by three people on different occasions and proclaim it, as Hamlet does, "very strange," adding that it "troubles" him. The prince, however, goes one step further. While pledging himself to become an eyewitness and to speak to the Ghost "if it *assume* [his] noble father's person," the man who has just conducted such a thorough examination of the evidence, left alone, exclaims:

My father's spirit—in arms! All is not well.
I doubt some foul play. Would the night were come.
Till then sit still, my soul. Foul deeds will rise,
Though all the earth o'erwhelm them, to men's eyes.

Suddenly, Shakespeare's hero appears less rigorous than Aeschylus's
Electra. He now seems to believe that the Ghost is his father's spirit itself
and from this to infer that something is wrong and that there is, or there
has been, "some foul play." Furthermore, he expresses total confidence
in the inevitable surfacing of "foul deeds" to human consideration. Yet
what "foul play" can Hamlet suspect and fear? And what "foul deeds"
can he so firmly believe in except for his mother's marriage to Claudius,
which needs no ghostly revelation? He seems to take the appearance of
the Ghost as a "sign" that "all is not well," then to build suspicion on it,
and finally to extract certainty out of the suspicion. What would Euripides have thought if Electra had done something like this, fabricating
knowledge through such "Pindaric" flights on the basis of such scanty
evidence?

Shakespeare supplies no direct answer to this question. Rather, he
seems to suggest an obscure, impalpable, and indefinite correspondence
between the inner "savoir" Hamlet has voiced earlier in the scene and
the cognition of mysterious new facts he has acquired from Horatio. "It
is not, nor it cannot come to good"; "All is not well": these are the two
statements in which Hamlet sums up what he knows before and after
Horatio's account of the Ghost, thus projecting one type of knowledge
onto the other and plunging us into an unprecedented state of epistemological mystery.

We expect some light from the encounter, announced as probable
and imminent, between Hamlet and the Ghost. What comes is indeed
light but surrounded by thicker darkness. As, during the night watch,
Hamlet disserts at length about the Danes' love of revel and drink, the
Ghost reappears. Halfway through scene iv of Act I, Hamlet sees and
addresses it, and we are convinced that a recognition scene will follow.
But the first words the hero speaks to what he knows looks exactly like
his father, are not of welcome. They concern its nature. Is this "a spirit
of health" or "a goblin damn'd," a good or an evil spirit? What interests
the enquiring mind of Hamlet is the Ghost's "questionable shape," the

fact that it has appeared in a form which requires interrogation and investigation. Hence, Hamlet chooses to speak to it and to *call* him "Hamlet, King, father, royal Dane." This is all the anagnorisis we are given: the subjective, voluntary attribution of a name in which are summed up the essential qualifications of the as yet unidentified entity that has appeared. And what kind of recognition can this be if Hamlet, as he proclaims, still "bursts in ignorance"? Like Horatio before him, Hamlet never asks the Ghost who he is; he rather implores an answer to "why," "what may this mean," "wherefore," and, finally and above all, "what should we do." The Ghost is for him an "it" (as Hamlet keeps saying throughout the scene) and a "dead corse." Yet Hamlet recognizes that what the "sepulchre" has "cast up again" is a "thou," that the "canoniz'd bones, hearsed in death" which have now "burst their cerements" were those of a person. The gnoseological question is identified with the essentially metaphysical mystery of death, the problem which Hegel asserts lies at the bottom of Hamlet's heart from the very beginning of the play. By revisiting the "glimpses of the moon" the Ghost makes night "hideous" but above all alters the "disposition," the mental constitution of men—who are but "fools of nature"—"with thoughts beyond the reaches of [their] souls." A ghost, Joyce's Stephen Dedalus says discussing *Hamlet,* is "one who has faded into impalpability through death, through absence, through change of manners." How can our souls, the souls of beings subject to the laws of nature, have thoughts that go beyond them to penetrate an "absence"? This is, basically, the problem Hamlet will return to time and again in the play, beginning with the famous "to be or not to be" monologue, where the "undiscover'd country, from whose bourn / No traveller [except ghosts!] returns" constitutes the central stumbling block. And yet what is thought, and in particular what can knowledge come to, if man's mental constitution does not allow him to go beyond the reaches of his soul—if all a human being tries to apprehend must already be within his mind's limits? Is *Hamlet,* by choosing the extreme case of the Ghost, proclaiming the impossibility of knowledge? We must go further in the play to see if this hypothesis is tenable, but before doing so let us pause a moment to consider yet another problem. When the Ghost refuses to answer Hamlet's questions and "waves" him "to a more removed ground," Horatio and Marcellus entreat the prince not to follow "it." Hamlet, who at this point cannot do without knowledge, replies that there is nothing to fear. He does not "set [his] life at a pin's fee," and as for his soul, "what can it do to that, / Being a thing immortal as itself?" What Hamlet, in an obviously Christian context, is saying, is that his own soul is as immortal as the Ghost, hence implying that the Ghost and his soul, that soul whose "reaches" are so limited by nature, have a fundamentally identical ontological status. Can there really be no communication, no knowledge between them?

Scene v provides Hamlet with knowledge but through revelation, not recognition. The Ghost promises to "unfold" something, proclaims Hamlet shall soon be bound to "revenge," and declares he is his father's spirit,

> Doom'd for a certain term to walk the night,
> And for the day confin'd to fast in fires,
> Till the foul crimes done in [his] days of nature
> Are burnt and purg'd away.

The Ghost's revelation is double. On the one hand, it concerns the murder of Hamlet's father by his brother Claudius (the account of which, incidentally, leaves totally uncertain the question whether the fratricide preceded or followed Claudius's winning of Gertrude "to his shameful lust" and makes no mention of her complicity with him). On the other hand, it tells Hamlet that his father is now a soul being "purg'd," presumably in Purgatory. In the first case, the Ghost's revelation agrees with Hamlet's inner awareness ("O my prophetic soul!")—so much so that some interpreters have followed Hegel in maintaining that "the apparition functions only as the objective for Hamlet's inner thought" (*des Innern*). In the second case, the Ghost tells Hamlet what his status after death is but, while mentioning its terrifying aspects, refuses to reveal its details because, he says, he is "forbid / To tell the secrets of [his] prison-house" and "this eternal blazon must not be / To ears of flesh and blood." Although the Ghost's reticence is justified by the dramatic effect it produces, his excuse would not be shared by contemporary spirits (as Andrea's in Kyd's *Spanish Tragedy*), let alone the souls of Dante's other world. The Ghost, in other words, deliberately maintains a degree of secrecy precisely about that "change of manners" of which Stephen Dedalus speaks and which is a fundamental problem for Hamlet as well.

Our hero, however, seems to accept his father's answers to his "why," "wherefore," and "what should we do" without questioning them. He pledges himself to revenge "with wings as swift / As meditation or the thoughts of love" and to "remember" the "poor ghost" "whiles memory holds a seat / In this distracted globe." Finally, pressed by the wonder of his fellow student Horatio and while humourously belittling the Ghost as a "boy," "truepenny," and "old mole," Hamlet draws the general conclusion out of the episode:

> There are more things in heaven and earth, Horatio,
> Than are dreamt of in your philosophy.

An apparently definitive statement of faith in "impalpability," supported and prompted by the spirit's voice, which continues to haunt the scene with an uncannily subterranean (and perhaps diabolical) ubiquity.

These, then, are the recognition and revelation scenes of *Hamlet*. How are we to interpret them, taking the foregoing pages into account? One thing we can say: Hamlet and the audience with him, while seemingly passing from ignorance to knowledge, do so in a completely unsatisfactory manner. We learn that the Ghost exists. As for its nature, meaning, purpose, and identity, we can only accept its undemonstrable words or rely upon vague clues such as a "likeness" which is never, and never can be, proved. Furthermore, we know there is a suspicious and mysterious correspondence between what I have called Hamlet's inner awareness and the knowledge the Ghost imparts to him. In a sense, we come close to the situation of Heisenberg's indeterminacy principle. At this level, the presence of the observer (Hamlet's consciousness) influences and alters the development of the phenomenon he is trying to understand (the Ghost's revelation) and thus makes it impossible to establish its nature and causes. There might indeed be more "things" in heaven and earth than our philosophy dreams of, but they are unknowable within the reaches of our souls—which, however, basically share the nature of those "things." This is one of the paradoxes that dominate *Hamlet*, particularly its recognition scenes.

·   ·   ·

This is also one of the reasons why a thoroughly rational, critical interpretation of those scenes is ultimately ineffable and why the best ever put forward comes not from a critic or a philosopher but from a creative writer. In one of the central episodes of Goethe's *Wilhelm Meisters Lehrjahre* Wilhelm and his company stage a production of *Hamlet*. Although they rehearse and discuss many details of the play before the *première,* Wilhelm pays no heed to the question of the Ghost. He has received a mysterious note which promises the actual presence of the Ghost on the scene at the right moment: "Your zeal deserves a miracle (*Wunder*). We cannot make miracles, but something marvellous (*Wunderbares*) shall happen." Wilhelm trusts the unknown writer. The evening of the performance, as the play begins, Wilhelm (whose role is that of Hamlet) is completing his makeup in front of a mirror when somebody runs in his dressing room crying, "The Ghost! The Ghost!" Startled but in a hurry to join the king and queen onstage, Wilhelm has no time to look around. When the curtain rises, Horatio approaches him and, "as if introducing himself," tells him: "The devil's inside the armour! He's terrified us all." In the interval, only two tall men wearing white mantles and hoods are visible in the wings, and Wilhelm, who feels his recitation of the first monologue has not been successful, enters the scene in a state of confusion. He pulls himself together, however, and goes through the passage on the Northerners' love of drinking "with appropriate indifference," forgetting the Ghost. He is, therefore, really terrified when Horatio cries, "Look, my Lord, it comes!"

> He jerked round, and the tall, noble figure, with its nimble inaudible step, the light movement in the heavy-looking armour, made such a strong impression on him that he stood there as if petrified and could only with a broken voice exclaim: "Angels and ministers of grace, defend us!" He stared at him, held his breath several times and pronounced the invocation to the Ghost in such a confused, broken, awkward manner that the greatest art could not have expressed it so well.

His own very literal translation of the passage helps him, and the audience is clearly fascinated. As it applauds wildly, the Ghost beckons and the prince follows him. The scene changes. When they reach the farthest place, the Ghost unexpectedly stops and turns. Hamlet, therefore, finds himself standing a little too near him. With longing and curiosity, Wilhelm tries then to look through the lowered beaver but can only discern deep-set eyes next to a well-shaped nose. Spying in trepidation, he stands before him. When from under the helm the first sounds come out and a voice, harmonious and only slightly hoarse, makes itself heard with the words, "I am thy father's spirit," Wilhelm withdraws a few steps in fear and the whole audience shivers. The voice seems known to everybody, and Wilhelm thinks he can notice a similarity to the voice of his father. These marvellous sensations and memories, the curiosity to discover the mysterious friend and the fear of offending him, the very unseemliness of coming too close to him as an actor in this situation, makes Wilhelm move alternately toward opposite sides of the scene. He changes position so often during the Ghost's long tale, he looks so uncertain and embarrassed, so attentive and yet so distracted, that his acting produces general admiration as the Ghost produces general terror. The spirit speaks with a deep feeling of discontent rather than despair—but "a spiritual, slow, unmeasurable discontent." It is the dejection of a great soul separated from all earthly things but which is subject to endless sufferings. Finally, the Ghost sinks down but in a singular fashion. A light grey, transparent veil which seems to rise like vapour from where he was sinking floats above him and then disappears with him under the stage.

The mounting suspense and the superimposition and interpenetration of theatrical fiction and reality (Hamlet–Wilhelm–William Shakespeare) in Goethe's passage constitute a very appropriate "translation" of Shakespeare, indeed a perfect example of the genius to improve an invention. Wilhelm has worked out all the details of *Hamlet,* yet the Ghost remains an unknown mystery both within and without the stage. It belongs to the sphere of *Wunder,* where the note of the mysterious friend has placed it, and all the company can do is "wait for the strangest guest role" (*wunderlichste Gastrolle*) to materialize. The status of the apparition is ambiguous and disconcerting. Horatio thinks it is the devil (as Hamlet will also fear in Shakespeare). In the wings—the world of reality— only two tall white figures are visible. Wilhelm sees two eyes and a nose, but, interestingly, the beaver of this Ghost is down and sight therefore uncertain. Furthermore, this detail has the power of raising suspicions about the Ghost of Shakespeare's Hamlet. He wears his beaver up when he appears to Horatio, but we are not told whether Hamlet can see his father's face at all. Finally, the recognition in *Wilhelm Meister* intensifies the eeriness of *Hamlet.* When the sounds of an harmonious and slightly hoarse voice emerge from the armour, the words that take shape are, "I am thy father's spirit." Shivering, both Wilhelm and the audience think they recognize the voice (*die Stimme schien jedermann bekannt*), but Wilhelm has an even more uncanny experience: he believes he can discern a "similarity" (*Ähnlichkeit*) to the voice of his own father.

The ontological depths sounded by this "likeness" (which cannot but recall Shakespeare's insistence on the same concept) between the voice of a mysterious actor impersonating a spirit—the voice of a real-unreal ghost—and that of an actor's—a man's—real father, find their counterpart in the epistemological uncertainty of Wilhelm's "impression" (*glaubte . . . zu bemerken*). The plane of the subject's "sensations" and "memories" (*Empfindungen und Erinnerungen*) is contiguous to and indeed made inescapably to intersect with that of his "curiosity" as a man and "preoccupation" as an actor, about the theatrical "situation." It is out of this insoluble compound of elements that the undefinable *Gestalt* of the father emerges—not just as Hegel's "objective form of Hamlet's inner mind," or only as Freud's "unconscious recognition" of a repressed impulse, but as a mysterious and complex *Ähnlichkeit* irrepressibly surfacing from the mind, from the theatre, from life. The scene ends as uncannily as it had begun, with a vapourlike veil disappearing under the stage. Interestingly enough, both the veil and the Ghost's mystery will haunt Wilhelm almost to the end of the novel and will never have a satisfactory explanation.

·   ·   ·

We all know what the encounter with the Ghost does to Shakespeare's Hamlet: how, having proclaimed the time "out of joint," he will consider it a "cursed spite" to have been born "to set it right," and how he will bear himself "strange or odd" "as [he] perchance hereafter shall think meet / To put an antic disposition on." I do not intend to follow all the numberless thematic threads of *Hamlet* but only those that bear on my topic, recognition. Of this, there seem to me three main parallel, intersecting, and yet diverging developments in the course of the tragedy. The first follows directly from the Ghost's revelation and concerns Hamlet's attempt at "proving" the spirit's story. The second is represented by Hamlet's growing recognition of his inaction. And the third is the sudden emergence of a new knowledge toward the end of the play.

Euripides' Orestes had asked himself and his sister whether the Apollo who ordered him to kill his mother might not be "a demon in likeness of the god." Likewise, Hamlet soon thinks that the spirit he has seen "may be a devil" who has "assumed" a "pleasing shape" to "abuse" and "damn" him. Whereas Orestes immediately overcomes his doubts, Hamlet decides to obtain proof of the Ghost's nature and of the truthfulness of his message. As he puts it, "I'll have ground / More relative than this." Hamlet's enquiry—his search for ultimate "recognition"— starts here. The mechanism he devises to acquire the decisive *semeion* is the play he has the actors stage, a play in which his father's supposed murder will be reenacted. Although he shows himself initially cautious about the certainty and efficacy of such a procedure ("I have *heard* / That guilty creatures . . . "), Hamlet immediately afterward expresses complete faith in the inevitability that "Murder, though it have no tongue, will speak / With miraculous organ." He will therefore "observe" his uncle's "looks": "I'll tent him to the quick. If a do blench, / I know my course." In short, "The play's the thing / Wherein [he]'ll catch the conscience of the king."

Hamlet's "reasoning" sounds impeccable, but in fact his language betrays a deep uncertainty in the links between the various stages of the *syllogismos*. In the first place, how precisely have "guilty creatures sitting at a play" "proclaimed their malefactions"? There is no doubt (although Hamlet only says "I have heard") that such criminals can be "struck to the soul" when beholding an "image" of their crimes. Modern fiction and modern police make use of similar methods. But how does Hamlet expect Claudius to confess? He—and this is the second point—would seem content that murder, even without a "tongue," will speak "with most miraculous organ." What kind of an organ might this be, and of what would its "miraculous" quality consist? Perhaps Hamlet means his uncle's "looks," his flinching. These certainly have no speaking tongue (they are mute signs), but they could hardly be said to be miraculous organs. Hamlet is looking for a "sign" but seems (quite understandably) uncertain as to its nature. Thus, while trying to gain "grounds more relative than this," that is to say, than the Ghost's revelation, he will take as "proof" the "conscience" of the king.

The conscience of Claudius might well be caught (as indeed it will), but a conscience cannot be taken as evidence. Hamlet seems to realize this, for when, before the actual performance of the play, he tells Horatio about his plan and asks him to "observe" his uncle "with the very comment of [his] soul," he replaces "conscience" by "speech":

If his [Claudius's] occulted guilt
Do not itself unkennel in one *speech,*
It is a *damned ghost* that we have seen,
And my *imaginations* are as foul
As Vulcan's stithy.

At the same time Hamlet promises he will "rivet" his eyes to Claudius's *face* and tells Horatio that afterward they shall "join" both their "judgments" "in censure of his *seeming*": he requires, then, a co-witness and a discussion of the evidence. This, however, has again become "seeming." Was the "speech" Hamlet a moment ago demanded the passage in the play he has himself composed, as some commentators would have it? Does "in" ("in one speech") really mean "at," "faced by"? The ambiguity of "tongue," "miraculous organ," "looks" in the preceding passage excludes this. Once more, I think, we are confronted by Hamlet's uncertainty and his reasonable wish to take all signs into account.

The dumb show is staged. The action reproduces, without words, Claudius's supposed murder of his brother by pouring poison in his ears and Claudius's wooing of Gertrude. Claudius does not flinch. The play follows. This time the actors speak, and, what is more, Hamlet himself provides a running commentary (he is "as good as a chorus," as Ophelia tells him). As, before the murder, the player Queen protests she will never be a wife if she ever becomes a widow, Claudius asks Hamlet if there is any "offence" in the "argument." The prince, taking "offence" as "crime," replies that "they do but jest—poison in jest" and goes on to explain that the play "is the image of a murder done in Vienna." When the future murderer appears on the stage, Hamlet glosses, "This is one Lucianus, nephew to the king." The action progresses to the poisoning of sleeping Gonzago. The king rises. His only words are, "Give me some light. Away." Hamlet turns to Horatio: "O good Horatio, I'll take the ghost's words / For a thousand pound. Didst perceive?" Horatio's two replies are "Very well, my lord," and, at Hamlet's insistence, "I did very well note him."

There clearly are several problems in this "recognition" scene. Hamlet accepts it as final proof of the Ghost's revelation, but all we hear from Claudius, after he voices his worry about the "offence," is a cryptic request for light, and all we hear from the co-witness, Horatio, is an astonishingly brief, neutral assent. The proof then depends on how the actor impersonating Claudius on the stage reacts through gesture rather than word to the murder being reenacted in a play within the play. Shakespeare gives us no indication of the way in which this reaction should be conveyed. Furthermore, we know that Claudius knows that the murderer in the play is not Gonzago's brother but his nephew—which would point to Prince Hamlet's revenge rather than to his uncle's crime as the reason for staging the play. Finally, we have the status itself of a theatrical performance. How can this relate to reality let alone mirror and prove it? In the monologue pronounced after the first player's recitation of Pyrrhus's murder of Priam and Hecuba, Hamlet had asked himself a central question:

> What's Hecuba to him, or he to her,
> That he should weep for her?

What does Hecuba, a fictional character, represent for the actor who talks about her? What is their relationship? The actor suits "his whole function" "with forms to his conceit": "And all for nothing! For Hecuba!" If Hecuba is no relation of the player, if fiction is "nothing" to reality, how can Hamlet expect a play to affect Claudius? Hamlet's question, however, presents a complementary aspect which is even more intriguing: "What's Hecuba to him, *or he to Hecuba?*" If "Hecuba" stands for "a character in fiction" and hence for fiction in general, does it make any sense to ask if reality means something to fiction, as the second part of Hamlet's question would seem to imply? If Hamlet is asking this question, we must conclude that he is subverting the established order of priorities, requiring not that "playing" should hold the mirror up to nature but that nature question itself in the mirror. The concept itself of reality is thus shattered to pieces.

In this context, knowledge—recognition of the Ghost's truthfulness by means of the right interpretation of Claudius's signs—becomes a nearly impossible task. *Hamlet* plunges us into this unbearable conundrum by showing us that never during the play does the prince obtain positive proof of Claudius's murder of his father (though he acquires evidence that the king intends to have *him* killed), whereas he, Hamlet, firmly believes in it after Claudius's reaction to the play and whereas the audience is actually shown how the king's conscience has indeed been pricked by the play. Claudius confesses his "offence," which "hath the primal eldest curse upon't," to heaven. We hear him; Hamlet does not.

Finally, *Hamlet* raises doubts which cannot be resolved as to the nature of the knowledge the prince accepts and, once more, as to the nature of the Ghost. When Hamlet talks to Gertrude in scene iv of Act III, he accuses his mother of having killed her husband, something the Ghost has never mentioned and which the text of the play nowhere justifies. Why Hamlet should bring this up remains a mystery. And why, in the same scene, the Ghost should be seen by the prince but not by Gertrude is also profoundly disturbing. Spirits can of course choose the people to whom they appear, but that they should be visible to some and simultaneously invisible to others is decidedly strange. Gertrude sees nothing, yet, as she says, she sees "all that is." Obviously, this constitutes no decisive indication that the Ghost is mere "vacancy," but it does cast a shadow of doubt over the whole question.

Hamlet's enquiry and the audience's reception of it become loose threads in midair. Questionable and contradictory, this first process of recognition is never completed. The bottomless depth is sounded once more by the prince when, in an apparently mere aside but in truth an oracular fashion, he proclaims that "to know a man well were to know himself." As a consequence of this jamming of the mechanism of knowledge, Hamlet's "reasoning"—quite unlike Electra's—endlessly circles around insoluble problems or crashes against unsurmountable walls. It is capable of organizing the logical premises of a *quaestio* on "to be or not to be" but cannot solve it because it comes upon the stumbling block of death and its unknowable realm and is forced to denounce "conscience" and declare that "thought" itself has a "pale cast." It is able to formulate the most astoundingly piercing double meaning and witty remarks, exposing truth to its bare bones, but neither Hamlet's interlocutors nor the audience really know whether this be in madness, in affectation of it, in folly with a "method," or a mixture of all. Finally, Hamlet's "reasoning" reaches a kind of degree zero when it is faced by the "absoluteness" of the grave digger's arguments. The circularity and speaking "by the card" of this character seem to prompt the prince out of "equivocation." His reasoning faultlessly follows the whole process of "likelihood" which through death and dust transforms Alexander the Great into loam stopping a beer barrel. Horatio himself, however, says

that "'Twere to consider too curiously to consider so." An excess of ingenuity, of minuteness brings Hamlet close to the emptiness of the grave
digger's "argal." Paradoxically, Hamlet's "curious" *syllogismos* is born out
of the one supreme recognition of the play. Aristotle had spoken of anagnorisis of "inanimate objects" (*apsykha*). Hamlet now recognizes Yorick's
skull. Here is the "mortal coil" reduced to grinning materiality. Here is
the "respect / That makes calamity of so long life"—a mute, abhorred,
base, smelly, "inanimate" object. This is the wall against which man's
"large discourse," his "capability and godlike reason," miserably crash.
Man's "looking before and after" can go back to Yorick's past "gambles"
on the one hand and forward to Alexander's clay on the other: beyond
these, no "discourse of reason" will ever reach.

In chapter 11 of the *Poetics,* Aristotle asserts that "it is possible to recognize whether one has acted or not." This kind of anagnorisis is present
throughout *Hamlet* and constitutes one of the prince's main torments.
Tragically, it continuously crosses with his failure at achieving empirical
and rational recognition of the Ghost and of Claudius's guilt. It is in fact
anagnorisis of his inaction that prompts Hamlet to devise a play which
he thinks will give him evidence against his uncle. Comparison with the
player's fiction triggers off this first moment of recognition:

> Yet I,
> A dull and muddy-mettled rascal, peak
> Like John-a-dreams, unpregnant of my cause,
> And can say nothing.

Like Pyrrhus in the player's story, Hamlet stands "like a neutral to his will
and matter." But his problem is that having recognized this, he does not
know why it should be so. Once more, a bottomless ignorance surfaces
out of anagnorisis:

> Now, whether it be
> Bestial oblivion, or some craven scruple
> Of thinking too precisely on th'event—
> A thought which, quartered, hath but one part wisdom
> And ever three parts coward—*I do not know*
> *Why* yet I live to say this thing's to do,
> Sith I have cause, and will, and strength, and means to do't.

Thus Hamlet's case, in Aristotelian terms, is that of a tragic character who, as we have seen at the beginning of this section, intends to act but refrains from acting and who recognizes his inaction but does not know to what it is due. There is no doubt that the Danish prince is right when he talks of the "fighting" in his heart and above all when he tells Guildestern that it is impossible to "pluck out the heart of [his] mystery."

That the heart of Hamlet—and of *Hamlet*—really is a mystery may be witnessed by the unexpected emergence of yet another form of recognition before the final catastrophe of the play. After Ophelia's funeral, during which the prince openly declares he loved her and for the first and only time proclaims himself "Hamlet the Dane," he discloses to Horatio Claudius's plot to have him killed in England. It is in this crucial first part of scene ii of Act V that Hamlet's new knowledge mysteriously surfaces. While telling Horatio how, aboard the ship for England, there was in his heart "a kind of fighting" and how he unsealed the "grand commission" of Rosencrantz and Guildestern, the prince comments that "indiscretion sometimes serves us well / when our deep plots do pall." Then, he adds

> and that should learn us
> There's a divinity that shapes our ends,
> Rough-hew them how we will—

Osric comes to announce the king's bet on Laertes' challenge. In the aside I have already noted Hamlet says that "to know a man well were to know himself." A lord summons the prince. As he leaves, Hamlet turns to Horatio: "Thou wouldst not think how ill all's here about my heart: but it is no matter." Horatio advises him to obey his foreboding by not fighting with Laertes. Hamlet's reply sums up this new type of recognition:

> Not a whit. We defy augury. There is special providence in the fall of a sparrow. If it be now, 'tis not to come; if it be not to come, it will be now; if it be not now, yet it will come. The readiness is all. Since no man, of aught he leaves, knows aught, what is't to leave betimes? Let be.

Where does the knowledge or wisdom expressed by Hamlet in this scene come from? We are unaware of its growing in his mind, and we are therefore invited to build our own story of its development outside the text. Second, one would not readily agree that the battle in Hamlet's heart is now over, as the fact that he asks Horatio whether it is "not perfect conscience / To quit" Claudius "with this arm" betrays a lingering sense of uncertainty. Furthermore, the "illness" about the prince's heart does not only refer to his presentiment, it also corresponds to his general state of mind throughout the play. And finally, while stating that knowledge of others is as unattainable as self-knowledge, Hamlet discerns a divinity which shapes our ends and a special providence in the fall of a sparrow. Once more we encounter in the hero's inner awareness and in the verbal fragments that voice it a series of contradictions and mysteries. We detect, as it were, the impossibility a human mind encounters when it tries to square the circle of knowledge—a circle the coordinates of which Hamlet perceives in flashes but which he cannot coherently order. The "I" is present in it, indeed hampers the process with his ill, mysterious essence. Knowledge of other human beings (the knowledge of anagnorisis in a play) appears as a line which, parallel to self-knowledge, runs ad infinitum, where we know they will meet but can never see them actually do so. On the other hand, one knows that human ends—the ends of those beings whose knowledge of themselves and of each other is constitutionally, inherently unreachable—are in some way shaped by a superior agency and that even chance occurrences like the fall of a sparrow are dominated by special providence. In this sense, Hamlet comes to the very particular form of recognition of *tykhonta*—the events that take place by chance—which Aristotle mentions in passing in chapter 11 of the *Poetics*. It is a poet's job, the philosopher says earlier on, "to report what is likely to happen; that is, what is capable of happening according to the rule of probability or necessity." This is tantamount to maintaining that tragedy represents chance as if ruled by purpose and thereby renders chance knowable. The unearthing of this knowledge constitutes the ultimate essence of tragic recognition. Hamlet, a character in a play, glimpses precisely this knowledge when he recognizes the work of purpose in human affairs and in the fall of a sparrow. He even "reasons" on this with his usual faultless logic, examining the three alternatives a human intellect can distinguish: "If it be now, 'tis not to come; if it be not to come, it will be now; if it be not now, yet it will come."

Hamlet expresses this knowledge in at least crypto-Christian terms, calling the agent of *tykhonta* "special providence" and alluding to the sparrows in Matthew's Gospel ("Are not two sparrows sold for a farthing? And one of them shall not fall on the ground without your Father"). At the same time, after uttering the words of wisdom and acceptance—"the readiness is all"—he goes far beyond Aristotle and Christianity. I have little doubt that given the premises in the entire play, in the last lines of Hamlet's present speech (which are notoriously uncertain from a textual viewpoint) human knowledge breaks down in final defeat, thus showing us the beginning of the end of Electra's, and our, Western "reasoning": "no man . . . knows aught."

CHAPTER TWO

In gentil hertes ay redy to repaire

Francesca and Troilus

The coupling of Francesca and Troilus is not merely the product of modern—particularly American—Chaucer criticism. It is at least as old as Romanticism. At the beginning of Book II of *Endymion* Keats proclaimed that

> The woes of Troy, towers smothering o'er their blaze,
> Stiff-holden shields, far-piercing spears, keen blades,
> Struggling, and blood, and shrieks—all dimly fades
> Into some backward corner of the brain;
> Yet, in our very souls, we feel amain
> The close of Troilus and Cressid sweet.

Keats had but to read *Inferno* V in Cary's version to be plunged into a dream which he called "one of the most delightful enjoyments" he had had in his life. He described this dream in an extraordinary sonnet which I believe is conclusive evidence that the story of Paolo and Francesca, itself precipitated by the reading of a book, in turn becomes the "galeotto" of modern culture and that the "myth" and "fiction" of courtly literature are there, in history, right at the beginning of modern consciousness:

As Hermes once took to his feathers light,
When lullèd Argus, baffled, swooned and slept,
So on a Delphic reed, my idle sprite
So played, so charmed, so conquered, so bereft
The dragon-world of all its hundred eyes;
And seeing it asleep, so fled away—
Not to pure Ida with its snow-cold skies,
Nor unto Tempe where Jove grieved that day;
But to that second circle of sad hell,
Where in the gust, the whirlwind, and the flaw
Of rain and hail-stones, lovers need not tell
Their sorrows. Pale were the sweet lips I saw,
Pale were the lips I kissed, and fair the form
I floated with, about that melancholy storm.

Keats may not be suspected of knowing anything about "courtly literature" or its more modern version, "courtly neurosis." At least seventy
years separate "As Hermes took" from Gaston Paris and one hundred
sixty from Henry Rey-Flaud, and the poet's reference to Troilus and Cressida in *Endymion* clearly shows that he had in mind Shakespeare's rather
than Chaucer's version. Yet the fascination which the two stories have for
Keats is something that, beyond any cultural scheme, we still feel. The
cause of that fascination is love, such as Keats himself viewed it when he
wrote in *Endymion*

Just so may love, although 'tis understood
The mere commingling of passionate breath,
Produce more than our searching witnesseth.

Love, "an orbèd drop of light," is not merely sensual passion but something which "genders a novel sense, / At which we start and fret, till in
the end, / Melting into its radiance, we blend, / Mingle, and so become
a part of it."

Both Dante and Chaucer, I think, would have understood this, and
this chapter tries to explain why and how they did so in their own cultural terms. A fundamental role in this explanation will be played by line
5 of Book III of Chaucer's *Troilus*, "in gentil hertes ay redy to repaire." The
line is the main title of this chapter because it has always intrigued me.

Why did Chaucer write it? We know the facts. In Boccaccio's *Filostrato,* Troiolo sings a Boethian hymn to Venus after the consummation of his affair with Criseida, at the end of Book III. Chaucer, who clearly recognizes the source behind that song in the *De Consolatione Philosophiae* II, metrum 8, turns one into two. He goes back directly to Boethius for Troilus's hymn, which will come at the end of Book III of *Troilus and Criseyde* with "Love, that of erthe and se hath governaunce." He moves the song of Boccaccio's Troiolo to the "Prohemium" or prologue to Book III, where it is pronounced not by a character in the story but by the authorial or narratorial voice itself.

At line 5 of the first stanza of Troiolo's song Chaucer finds the following expression as one of the attributes of Venus: "benigna donna d'ogni gentil core" (benign lady of every "gentle," i.e., noble, heart). Instead of translating that line, which points to Venus's beneficent lordship over every noble heart, Chaucer—apparently out of the blue— inserts his version of the *incipit* of Guido Guinizzelli's canzone, "Al cor gentile rempaira sempre amore": *in gentil hertes ay redy to repaire.* As usual when he does this kind of thing, Chaucer adds no explanation, and as the line fits in perfectly well with the rest of the stanza we give it no further thought and read on.

But it is one thing to say that Venus, the light both "blisful" and "eternal" which adorns the entire third heaven, the sun's beloved and Jove's daughter—the goddess, in other words, as well as the planet—is the "domina" or Lady of every noble heart and another to call her "plesance of love" and "goodly debonaire" and then see her as always ready to "repaire," that is, to return to the noble heart as to her home. Chaucer's stanza begins, as it were, in the third heaven and ends in the human heart. Both are, to borrow an expression from his own *House of Fame,* the "kyndely stedes" of Love's light: one in the cosmos, one in the human being (as Petrarch classically formulates it in a ballad, "Amor, che 'n cielo e 'n gentil core alberghi"). The change may seem minor, but I think that in the context of the *Troilus* it is in fact momentous.

To explain why this is so, I embark on a tortuous and slightly heretical journey, during which I read an intertext which covers the period from the late thirteenth to the end of the fourteenth century—a period I would call the age of "belated" *courtoisie.* The movement I follow is from lyric to narrative and goes through three main stages: first, analogy and metaphysics; second, interpretation, allegory, and metamorphosis; third, reading and back to analogy. In other words, here the "improvement" on the original invention will be seen to cross the boundaries between literary genres and to intermingle with different ways of thinking, of approaching reality itself.

The first step to take on this long route obviously is to go back to Guinizzelli's canzone. As everyone knows, in this justly famous poem the Bolognese writer set out to illustrate the relationship between love and the noble heart—a theme which was central to the general European meditation about courtly love, particularly to Italian ideas of it. Compared with his predecessors, Guinizzelli frames traditional concepts within a more coherent, logical, and "scientific" whole while at the same time colouring them linguistically and imaginatively in a completely new manner. The result is what people have taken it to be for over seven hundred years: a manifesto not so much of a new doctrine but precisely of a new style, the Stil Nuovo. Yet "style" does not simply mean a way of writing; it clearly implies an "approach" as well. And Guinizzelli's approach is new enough. "Andreas Capellanus," that elusive devil to whose De Amore everything pertaining to courtly love once seemed to go back, had seen "morum probitas," or nobility, as the sufficient motivation or basis of love ("*acquirit* amorem in morum probitate fulgentem"). But Guinizzelli goes one step further. He puts forward a universal law of love, a law which obtains everywhere and always ("sempre"—Chaucer was to render this with "ay"). His is indeed a "metaphysics" of love, and the discourse which illustrates it is appropriately based on analogy:

> Al cor gentile rempaira sempre amore
> come l'ausello in selva a la verdura.
> (Love always returns home to the noble heart
> like a bird to the green leaves in a wood.)

Nature did not create love before the noble heart, or the noble heart before love. As soon as the sun came into being ("fu"), the splendour of light came into being, nor did it exist before the sun. And love takes its place (has its "kyndely stede") in nobility as naturally ("propiamente") as heat in the clarity, the brightness of fire. The ontology is founded upon an analogy not only with the animal world of everyday experience (the bird that returns to the forest green) but also with the very beginning of things, the "principia rerum": sun and light. When the Big Bang was, we might paraphrase, love was; simultaneously, the Big Bang's radiation also was. The "cor gentile" is this radiance ab initio. "Love," wrote Emily Dickinson, "is anterior to Life - / Posterior to Death - / Initial of Creation and - / the Exponent of Earth."

Guinizzelli continues, going through the entire natural world and the four elements—fire, water, earth, air; precious stones, stars, diamonds, "rivera," mud, sky—and concentrating on images of brightness. For five stanzas he proposes one analogy after the other, each time repeating and varying one or more elements from the preceding comparison. Thus, to quote a few lines that will be useful later on:

Foco d'amore in gentil cor s'aprende
come vertute in petra preziosa
(The fire of love is kindled in the noble heart
like virtue in a precious stone)

Amor per tal ragion sta 'n cor gentile
per lo qual foco in cima del doplero
(Love stands in the noble heart in the same manner
as fire at the top of a torch)

In spite of its apparent static quality, the poem is an extraordinary tour de force. Along this analogic spiral, in fact, we move only two steps beyond the initial statement—in stanza 3, when we are told that the lady, like a star, "innamora" the heart elected and made noble and pure by nature; and in stanza 5, where the theory that nobility comes as family heritage is refuted. This stanza ends with the two wonderful images of the water that "carries," or lets itself be penetrated by, the ray of light and the sky that "retains" the unalterable splendour of the stars. Suddenly, then, in stanza 6 the poet leaps from sky to heaven, from one "cielo" to another. God the Creator, he writes, shines before the angelic intelligence of heaven more than the sun does to our eyes. That intelligence knows ("intende") its Creator beyond heaven and, in moving heaven, begins to obey Him. In the manner in which the completion of the act disposed by the just God instantly follows that intuition ("in-tention"), so, truly, the beautiful lady, when she shines in the eyes of her noble servant, should communicate to him such a desire that he would never want to stop obeying her:

Splende 'n la 'ntelligenzia del cielo
Deo criator più che ['n] nostr'occhi 'l sole:
ella intende suo fattor oltra 'l cielo,
e 'l ciel volgiando, a Lui obedir tole;
e con' segue, al primero,
del giusto Deo beato compimento,
così dar dovria, al vero,
la bella donna, poi che ['n] gli occhi splende
del suo gentil, talento
che mai di lei obedir non si disprende.

Clearly, we have gone a step further. At the beginning of the poem, Nature makes the sun, love, and the noble heart. Here, we see God as Creator shining in the angelic intelligence—moving, as Aristotle would put it, by being loved. We are *before* the Big Bang, and the metaphysics acquires the hues of religion. Indeed, from the beginning we are then immediately brought to the end, beyond death, to the last things, to Doomsday. In the last stanza, the poet's soul stands before God for the final judgement, and God reproaches it: "What have you dared to do? You have passed beyond heaven and come to Me, and yet you took Me only as a simile for vain love (e desti in vano amor Me per semblanti). To Me is praise due, and to the Queen of the venerable kingdom, through whom all deception vanishes."

God's accusation is directed not simply against idolatry but against its very basis, that analogy which has dominated the poem so far and which, pushed to the extreme, brings the poet to take God Himself as a mere "semblanti," a term of comparison, for "vain love." In other words, the poet stages here the fundamental Christian indictment of courtly love and courtly *literature*. I would go as far as to say that it was this moment of self-consciousness and self-criticism, as well as the poet's bold, ironical, genial reply, that, in Dante's eyes, saved Guinizzelli from Hell and destined him to Purgatory. "She bore the semblance of an angel belonging to Your kingdom," he rejoins the Creator, "it was no fault of mine (non me fu fallo) to place my love in her." The error consisted, the poet seems to say, not in taking God's "semblanti" for "vain love" but in a far lesser analogical mistake, that of falling in love with the lady's *angelic* "semblanza."

In short, in "Al cor gentile" we have the fascinating dramatization of a whole culture—and this takes place in two ways, by images and by movement. By way of images, we pass from Boethius to courtly literature. For, if the lady's angelic appearance at the end of the poem is a conceit common enough in the love poetry of the Troubadours and their Italian descendants, the first simile of Guinizzelli's poem is definitely Boethian. In the *Consolatio*, Book III, metrum 2 (here quoted in Chaucer's own translation), Philosophy decides to "shewe by subtil soong, with slakke and delytable sown of strenges, how that Nature, myghty, enclyneth and flytteth the governementz of thynges, and by whiche lawes sche, purveiable, kepith the grete world; and how sche, byndynge, restreyneth alle thynges by a boond that may nat be unbownde." One of the main examples she uses to prove how "alle thynges rejoysen hem of hir retornynge ayen to hir nature" (i.e., of their "repairing" home) is that of the bird which, if imprisoned in a cage, "seketh mornynge oonly the wode, and twytereth desyrynge the wode with hir swete voys": "come l'ausello in selva a la verdura."

There are two complementary movements in Guinizzelli's poem. If one reads it from beginning to end, one finds a progress in nature from the animal world to the sky and then to heaven; then, beyond death and nature, to God. But if one reads the poem backward as the poet himself invites us to do in stanza 6, the movement is from God to the angelic intelligence and hence, analogically, to the lady and the noble heart, on the one hand, and to the sky, earth, water, fire—in sum, the natural world—on the other. The agent of this double movement is love, in its Boethian, cosmic aspect of "amor quo caelum regitur" (of which that love which returns home to the noble heart is an essential feature in the world of men) and in its aspect of love for God, Who moves by being loved (of which man's love for a lady is an analogy).

.   .   .

No wonder, then, that Dante considered "Al cor gentile" a manifesto of the new poetry and constantly returned to it in his own works. And it is through Dante's versions of Guinizzelli's poem that we have to go in order to reach Chaucer, the reasons being both strictly philological (Chaucer may have known the first line of the poem through Dante) and, as we shall see presently, more general and philosophical. Dante uses "Al cor gentile" in three different ways: first, he quotes it for purposes of illustration or as an authority; second, he adapts it in his treatment of specific themes or scenes; third, he echoes it or employs it as an underlying echo to signal key moments in his own development as a poet or, in the *Comedy,* fundamental stages in his own progress as a character.

In the *De Vulgari Eloquentia* (II, v, 4), for instance, Guinizzelli's famous *incipit* is quoted as an example of the "most superb" kind of verse, the endecasillabo, or eleven-syllable line. In Tractate IV of the *Convivio* (xx, 7)—a part of the work which Chaucer certainly knew—"Al cor gentile rempaira sempre amore" and the analogy with the precious stone's "virtual power" find their place in the context of a general discussion of "gentilesse" and in particular of its being "infused" by God into man's soul. In a sonnet of the *Vita Nuova* (XX, 3), on the other hand, Dante, who had apparently been asked by Cavalcanti to produce a definition of love, invokes Guinizzelli ("il saggio") as an authority but from the very beginning of the poem goes one small, yet significant step further than his predecessor. Love and the noble heart were distinct, though inseparable, in "Al cor gentile." In Dante, they become *one* thing: the one can no more exist without the other than a rational soul without reason (and the analogy is indeed significant, given Dante's conception of love as an impulse engaging the higher as well as the lower powers of the soul):

> Amore e 'l cor gentil sono una cosa,
> sì come il saggio in suo dittare pone,
> e così esser l'un sanza l'altro osa
> com'alma razional sanza ragione.

Nature, Dante continues, creates love and the noble heart at the same time, "love as the lord and the heart as his mansion," but love lies asleep in the heart until it is awakened by the lady's beauty. "The genesis of love," Foster and Boyde comment, "is this awakening: not something new or extraneous, but a movement from *potentia* to *actus,*" as Dante himself glosses a few lines later. This is Dante's "major—and in spirit very Aristotelian—modification of the views of earlier theorists": it is one of the ways in which he shows his genius to improve an invention. From the very beginning, his poetry (and we are talking specifically of love poetry) takes a philosophical turn. But we must also note a few more features of Dante's use of "Al cor gentile."

First, in the *Vita Nuova* this sonnet comes immediately after the great canzone "Donne ch'avete intelletto d'amore," which marks the opening of a wholly new phase of Dante's poetry, that of Beatrice's "loda," or praise. And "Donne ch'avete" contains, from its very opening, several echoes of Guinizzelli's penultimate stanza ("intelligenzia"—"intelletto").

Second, this moment is a very particular one in the narrative of the *Vita Nuova*—a moment of happiness both personal and poetic, in which, as Dante says of the first line of "Donne ch'avete," his tongue speaks as if moved by itself. Only three chapters later Dante is ill and dreams of Beatrice's death, and eight chapters after "Amore e 'l cor gentil" Beatrice actually dies. Dante "sacrifices" Beatrice, killing her to life in order to elevate her to Heaven and internalize her as part of his memory. This momentous murder-cum-translation, this submitting the beloved to death, changes Dante's life and poetry forever by gradually bringing his sighs "oltre la spera che più larga gira," beyond the ninth heaven, to the Empyrean, to a new understanding of love—to an "intelligenza nova" of courtly culture—and to the "mirabile visione" which makes him decide not to speak of the blessed lady until he will be able to say about her things never spoken of any other woman, bringing him, in short, to the end of the *Vita Nuova* and the beginning of a shadow that will become the *Comedy* and the germ of the *Paradiso*.

Third, Dante stamps his own mark on Guinizzellian poetry. He does not try to adapt the Bolognese writer's first line, but, following rather the first and third sentences of "Al cor gentile"'s third stanza ("Amor per tal ragion sta 'n cor gentile" and "Amore in gentil cor prende rivera"), he opens his sonnet with the appropriate subject, Love: not "*Al cor gentile rempaira sempre amore*" but "*Amore e 'l cor gentil sono una cosa.*" This emphasis will remain constant throughout Dante's poetry, in which the anaphoric openings with "Amor" form a beautiful string of para-Guinizzellian lyrics: "Amor che ne la mente mi ragiona" in *Convivio* II; "Amor, ch'al cor gentil ratto s'apprende" in *Inferno* V; "Amore, / acceso di virtù, sempre altro accese" in *Purgatorio* XXII. Moreover, as scholars have convincingly shown, the presence in Dante of Guinizzelli's "Al cor gentile" is even more pervasive. The bird imagery of "come l'ausello in selva a la verdura" is picked up and intensified in *Inferno* V, in *Purgatorio* XXIV, and in *Purgatorio* XXVI, that is to say, whenever in the *Comedy* Dante speaks about love or poetry or both. Last but not least, Guinizzelli's fifth stanza ("Splende 'n la 'ntelligenzia del cielo") clearly inspires two of Dante's most important canzoni, "Donne ch'avete intelletto d'amore" in the *Vita Nuova* and "Voi che intendendo il terzo ciel movete" in the second book of the *Convivio*.

I have no space here to deal with each of these compositions in detail, but I would like to make three points about them. They signal key moments in Dante's development as a man by using substantially the same kind or "style" of poetry but *interpreting* it as something different. "Voi che intendendo" is addressed to the angelic spirits that move the heaven of Venus and describes a conflict in Dante's heart between the claims on his love of two women: one, Beatrice, "in possession" when the conflict begins; the other, identified by Dante in *Convivio* II as Philosophy, virtually winning when the conflict ends. This is, then, a turning point in the poet's life. But literarily it is presented to us in a poem which preserves the language and framework of Dante's earlier love poetry, yet relies on allegory to yield its full meaning. "Amor che ne la mente mi ragiona" employs the very same "praise style" in which Dante had hymned the beauty of Beatrice in the *Vita Nuova* with "Donne ch'avete intelletto d'amore," but the lady celebrated here, as *Convivio* III explains, is Philosophy, conceived as a total dedication of intellect and will to the divine Wisdom revealed in the cosmic order and in man's own nature—a *figura* whose chief sources are Boethius's *Consolatio* and the Sapiential books of the Old Testament. I shall quote four lines of this magnificent poem to give an idea of how Dante operates. He is describing the lady's appearance:

> Cose appariscon ne lo suo aspetto
> che mostran de' piacer di Paradiso,
> dico ne li occhi e nel suo dolce riso,
> che le vi reca Amor com'a suo loco.
> (In her aspect things appear
> that show the joys of Paradise
> —I mean in her eyes and her lovely smile;
> for it is there, as to the place which belongs
> to him, that Love leads them.)

When he starts commenting on this canzone in *Convivio* III, Dante writes that his "second love had its beginning, its source, in the merciful 'sembianza' of a lady." In other words, we are witnessing the momentous transformation of Guinizzellian analogy into Dantean allegory. The *poetry* is still analogical, as the lines I have just quoted show. But the interpretation of the poetry—the reading, as it were, of the "sembianza"—is allegorical. However, the two are, particularly in the case of "Amor che ne la mente mi ragiona," inseparable. Dante, as he himself says at the beginning of the *Convivio,* does not recant the sweet new style. He simply analyzes it, and as a glossator and commentator creates a wholly new literature—a literature which is still courtly but in which the court itself is moving from the Palace (or the streets of Florence) to the "schools" of clerics and philosophers, shortly to become the "court" of Heaven. An "improvement" of this kind amounts to a revolution.

True, the final part of the *Convivio* such as we have it indicates a seemingly definitive decision to abandon the "sweet rhymes of love" and to use new, harsh, and subtle verses of *rectitudo.* But in the *Comedy,* where the conversion to ethics that underlies the poetic crisis of the *Convivio* becomes the source itself of inspiration, the old love poetry comes back once more. In fact, it is quite deliberately rearranged in a sequence which spans from the first circle of Hell through Purgatory up into the third heaven. Here is Francesca proclaiming, "Amor, ch'al cor gentil ratto s'apprende" in *Inferno* V. Then, Casella sings "Amor che ne la mente mi ragiona" in *Purgatorio* II. In *Purgatorio* XXIV, the poet Bonagiunta sees Dante and asks him if he really is the man who created the "new rhymes," inaugurating the "dolce stil novo" with his "Donne ch'avete intelletto d'amore." In *Purgatorio* XXVI, Dante meets Guido Guinizzelli himself and celebrates his "dolci detti" and the "uso moderno" as well as the poetry of Arnaut Daniel. Finally, in *Paradiso* VIII, Charles Martel introduces himself and his companions as the spirits who "revolve with the celestial Princes" of the Heaven of Venus whom—he says—Dante had addressed with his "Voi che 'ntendendo il terzo ciel movete." This sequence must have a meaning. And I think the meaning can be summed up in the grandiose metamorphosis and apotheosis which courtly love undergoes in Dante's hands by way of a progressive, narrative, and contextual sublimation of an earlier lyrical phase through death. The movement completes and fully christianizes the ascending progress of

Guinizzelli's analogies. It saves courtly literature by rereading it, by seeing it as one mode of discourse in the universal *langage* of eros—of desire, of *love:* of love between human beings, of love for knowledge and wisdom, of love for God. Think of the progress in the *Comedy:* the lustful in Hell; the penitent lustful in Purgatory; then, in Paradise, the spirits of those who, under the influence of Venus, burnt with love on earth. Love is what they all have in common. I know, of course, that as cantos XVII–XVIII of *Purgatorio* make clear, there are crucial differences. While "natural love," that is, the love by which all things are inclined by nature toward their proper place or goal, is "always without error"—as Virgil tells Dante there—"elective love" or "love of the mind" may indeed err, either by turning to an evil object or by having too much or too little vigour. This kind of love is subject, then, to free choice, and this means that in Dante's eyes the direction it takes may ultimately bring man to either Hell or Heaven.

Still, love is love, and I think that only in the context of its unity as well as of its diversity can we understand Francesca. Francesca has been taken as an *exemplum* of carnal sin par excellence, as the paradigm of those "who submit reason to pleasure," and as both the vindicator and the victim of courtly love and its literature. By having Francesca recount her tragic end and placing her in Hell—critics say—Dante himself expiates her sin and definitively condemns that kind of love and that kind of literature. If it were so, then I do not see why Dante went on quoting Stil Nuovo poetry all the way to Paradise and why he staged the great recognition scene with Beatrice in the Garden of Eden. Francesca, I think, shows us in the first place how love between two human beings of different sexes is born.

Here we are, then. We have passed beyond the horrible, snarling Minos who dispatches damned souls to their circle in Hell by turning his tail's spires. We have, with Keats, entered darkness and the hurricane of winds. The souls of carnal sinners, of those who "subjected reason to desire," are swept along by the storm like starlings in the cold season, like cranes making long lines in the air and chanting their lays. Here are the shades of the ladies and knights of old vanquished by love— pagans like Achilles, Paris, and Helen and Christians like Tristan. Dante, overcome by pity and "quasi smarrito," spots two souls which, light on the wind, go together led by love and calls out to them. At his cry, they come closer. And we have a first surprise. For the simile Dante uses to describe the approach of the two shades is basically Virgilian, but also I think undoubtedly reminiscent of Guinizzelli's "come l'ausello in selva a la verdura" and its antecedent in Boethius's *Consolatio:*

> Quali colombe dal disio chiamate
> con l'ali alzate e ferme al dolce nido
> vegnon per l'aere dal voler portate

The doves are called by desire and are borne by their will through the air, with wings poised and motionless, to their *sweet nest.* They "repair" home, to their "kyndely stede." And the appointed place to which they are drawn by eros is the nest of *love.* The two souls—the two "gentil hertes"—are brought back to the primeval feeling: *disio, amor.* When one of them, a woman's voice in the silence of wind, starts speaking, it is to that feeling she almost immediately returns. Francesca picks up the Guinizzellian echo of the preceding simile and recounts how love between two human beings explodes in a sudden conflagration, a *coup-de-foudre:*

> Amor, ch'al cor gentil ratto s'apprende,
> prese costui della bella persona
> che mi fu tolta; e 'l modo ancor m'offende.
> Amor, che a nullo amato amar perdona,
> mi prese del costui piacer sì forte,
> che, come vedi, ancor non m'abbandona.
> Amor condusse noi ad una morte.
> Caina attende chi a vita ci spense.
> (Love, which is quickly kindled in the noble heart,
> seized this man for the fair form
> that was taken from me, and the manner afflicts me still.
> Love, which absolves no one beloved from loving,
> seized me so strongly with his charm,
> that, as you see, it does not leave me yet.
> Love brought us to one death.
> Caina waits for him who quenched our life.)

Man and his noble heart, the physical beauty of the woman, his love. Love irresistibly returned by the woman with everlasting, strong delight. Note how Francesca subtly changes Guinizzelli by turning not to the first line of his canzone but to line 11, "Foco d'amor in gentil cor s'aprende." Not love that repairs home to the noble heart, but a fire that is kindled there violently and quickly—*ratto*. Moreover, this allows no analogy with the virtual power of a precious stone but rather points to the sudden seizure of the male heart by the female's "bella persona." Francesca pushes Guinizzelli to the extreme. She "improves" on him by misreading him, turning his analogies into cause–effect relationships and his metaphysics into a phenomenology.

She further misinterprets Guinizzelli by adding to the sudden "aprendere" of one heart the other's inevitable "response," for which she seems to draw on the *De Amore* ("amor nil posset amori denegare"). It is this "attraction fatale" that Francesca powerfully sketches in with her triple anaphora. It is its inevitability, which kills free choice and from which she is unable to escape even now, that led both—fatally indeed— to death. Not to the trial of Guinizzelli's soul before God, or to Dante's ritual sacrifice and translation of Beatrice in the *Vita Nuova*, but to being murdered, judged by Minos and condemned to Hell.

Let me point out that, no matter how much I would like to do so, I am not pleading not guilty for Francesca. For Dante, she and Paolo *are* guilty. They subjected reason to desire, they committed adultery, they are in Hell. What I am defending is human *love*, the force of which both Dante and each one of us know quite well. The "attraction" I see as vital, its sudden explosion as dangerous, its inevitability as wrong and fatal.

By justifying love—the feeling that joins two human beings—I save "courtoisie" and courtly literature the way Dante saved them. Francesca, I said, misreads Guinizzelli. It isn't the only misreading in her story. When, after Dante's sad meditation on the two lovers' "sweet thoughts" and "great desire," Francesca leaves general principles and gets to the facts, to the manner in which Love granted them actual knowledge of the "dubbiosi disiri"—to what she calls its "first root"—she quotes Boethius (this time correctly) and then proceeds to relate the famous story of the reading session with Paolo. One day, she says, they were read- ing of Lancelot's falling in love. Alone and without any suspicion, they went on, their eyes often brought to meet and their faces deprived of colour by that "lettura." One point finally overcame them, and that was when they read how the "disiato riso," the desired, smiling lips of

Guinevere, were kissed by Lancelot. At that moment Paolo, trembling, kissed Francesca's mouth. The book and its author, she adds, were true Galehaults, that is, true pandars. And, she concludes, that day we read no further in it.

The fact is, however, that in the prose *Lancelot du Lac* to which Francesca is referring it is Guinevere who, persuaded by Galehault, kisses Lancelot and not the other way around. Once more, then, Francesca misreads a text—this time, precisely while reading it—and once more this text is courtly literature. She is not just, as Contini memorably put it, "un'intellettuale di provincia," a provincial intellectual. Francesca is a dangerous misreader of courtly literature. In a subtle way, Dante himself has pointed this out. For the "disiato riso" of *Inferno* V he saw—as we noticed above—on the lips of Philosophy in "Amor che ne la mente mi ragiona" and in the *Convivio,* and will see on those of Beatrice in *Purgatorio* XXXII:

> Tant'eran li occhi miei fissi e attenti
> a disbramarsi la decenne sete,
> che li altri sensi m'eran tutti spenti.
> Ed essi quinci e quindi avien parete
> di non caler—così lo *santo riso*
> a sé traéli con l'antica rete!—
> (So fixed and intent were my eyes
> in satisfying their ten-year thirst,
> that every other sense was quenched in me.
> And they themselves had a wall of indifference,
> on one side and on the other, so did the holy smile
> draw them to itself with the old net.)

Furthermore, in both the canzone and *Paradiso* XVIII (where Beatrice tells a transfixed Dante, "non pur ne' miei occhi è paradiso"), the Lady's eyes and smile are presented as "figures" of Paradise. But it is up to us to see them as such. If we do not misread, but read the smile analogically, allegorically, and poetically, we will be able to understand the continuity and transformation signalled by the "disiato" of *Inferno* V, the "dolce" of *Convivio* III, and the "santo" of *Purgatorio* XXXII, all tied together by the supreme smile of the beloved. If we do not do this, if we do not look at love from beyond earth and death, we become victims of lust and of fatalism. We read our books wrongly and end up in Hell.

Yet to pursue this sublimation is not at all easy but in fact painful and lacerating. Dante knows how difficult—indeed, for some impossible—it is to grasp the continuity, to create the metamorphosis within oneself. His "pietà" dominates the canto and in the end prompts his swoon at Francesca's words and Paolo's tears. In canto II, he had called his visit to Hell the "*war* of pity" (guerra de la pietate). This conflict— the tragic *eleos* of Aristotle's *Poetics*—explodes in the last three lines of *Inferno* V to the point of making Dante the spectator, who falls down "like a dead body," experience a "closing" of the mind (canto VI) and a form of death. Perhaps he is suggesting that while human pity overcomes us when we hear such beautifully conflicting tales, we should succumb and die in order to "translate" them onto a higher sphere.

•   •   •

I think that one of the few people who understood Dante's reading of the Guinizzellian message and interpreted it with originality was Geoffrey Chaucer. First, Chaucer felt the importance of pity so much that five times in his works he significantly replaced Francesca's "amor" with "pitee" in the formulation, "pitee renneth soone in gentil herte." That this line constitutes a "translation by assonance" from *Inferno* V should be beyond doubt. The two sequences, "renneth soone" and "gentil herte," are perfectly, chiastically equivalent to "ratto s'apprende" and "al cor gentile." Chaucer substitutes "pitee" for "love" not because in the code of "gentilesse" they are synonyms but precisely in order to underline the difference between them, a difference that looks the greater the more one considers the two notions as contiguous. Second, Chaucer saw quite clearly the connection between *eros* and *thanatos* powerfully suggested by *Inferno* V. In the *Parliament of Fowls* he provides us with a list, drawn from both the *Teseida* and *Inferno* V, of people whose destiny was love-and-death. The list includes Semiramis, Cleopatra, Achilles, Helen, Paris, Tristan (thus far following Dante), and then Isolde and Troilus.

In a sense, then, from the very beginning Chaucer sees Troilus in a Dantean perspective. This perspective is widened and deepened in *Troilus and Criseyde*. On the one hand, we have the metaphorical parabola that brings Troilus from looking like a flower opening up before the bright sun in Book II to resembling a tree bare of all its leaves in Book IV—a parabola which begins with the hopeful joy of Dante in *Inferno* II and ends with the fatal despair of the damned flocking to Charon's boat in *Inferno* III. On the other hand, we are invited by the initial lines of *Troilus* II, which contain a clear echo of the *Purgatorio*'s opening, to read Book II of the poem as a kind of Purgatory, Books I and III being presented more obliquely, through several allusions and the poetic invocations to the infernal Fury, Thesiphone, and to Venus and Calliope, as respectively a Hell and a Paradise.

Third, the stories of Paolo and Francesca and of Dante and Beatrice are constantly evoked and counterpointed. Let us look, first, at Troilus's love for Criseyde. Can anyone find a better description of its beginning than Francesca's lines, "Amor, ch'al cor gentil *ratto* s'apprende, prese *costui*"? Love "renneth" as "soone" as an arrow to the heart of Troilus. The word "sodeynly" is repeated twice at the very beginning of Book I, and the laws of Love and Nature resonantly proclaimed immediately afterward by the Narrator:

> For evere it was, and evere it shal byfalle,
> That Love is he that alle thing may bynde,
> For may no man fordon the lawe of kynde.

Later in Book I, Troilus, following Boccaccio's Troiolo, will himself echo Francesca's second terzina, "Amor, ch'a nullo amato amar perdona," "improving" it:

> Love, ayeins the which whoso defendeth
> Hymselven most, hym alderlest avaylleth

Francesca's love for, and delight in, Paolo never abandon her ("che, come vedi, ancor non m'abbandona"). The same is true of Troilus who, at least while alive, cannot "unlove" Criseyde, not even for "a quarter of a day." In the meantime, we will have noticed that if, in Dantean terms, Troilus begins by resembling Paolo, in the course of the poem he increasingly becomes like Francesca—an inversion of roles which is significant in the perspective of both the general "feminisation" of the courtly knight noted by Kenelm Foster and the particular "feminisation" of this hero

brilliantly described by Jill Mann. Accordingly, it is Criseyde who, thus
returning to a faithful reading of the *Lancelot*, kisses Troilus first, the
manoeuvres of Pandarus bringing about the same success that crown
those of Galehault.

Does Criseyde in any way fit into this Dantean frame? If Dante
Alighieri were reading the *Troilus* he would certainly be surprised to follow the dialogue between Pandarus and Criseyde one-third of the way
through Book II. Pandarus is trying to persuade his niece not to bind
herself to Troilus but to "make hym bettre chiere." Criseyde listens attentively, decides to discover what her uncle means, and asks him, "Well,
what would you suggest? What would you advise me to do about this?"
And Pandarus, unlike his equivalent in the *Filostrato*, replies:

> Certein, best is
> That ye hym love ayeyn for his lovynge,
> As love for love is skilful guerdonynge.

Here we are, Dante would think, that's it! This is my Francesca's "Amor,
ch'a nullo amato amar perdona." Sure, the romantic fatalism of the original sentence has been replaced by English sense ("best is"), by reason-
ableness ("skilful"). But the lines seem to have the unmistakable ring of
the *De Amore,* the stamp of "Andreas Capellanus." Yes. However transformed from that inevitable nonsparing ("perdona") into a reasonable
rewarding ("guerdonynge"), the rule is Francesca's: "That ye hym love
ayeyn for his lovynge." Well done, Dante would say, enough is kept,
enough is changed. The invention is properly improved. This is going
to be a Francesca-like story, beautiful and tragic.

Yet Dante would only have to read two hundred lines further to find
that the English poet is of a quite different persuasion. Pandarus seems
to assume that the moment Criseyde will belong to Troilus ("whan ye
ben his al hool as he is youre") is drawing near. But she stops him: "Nay,
therof spak I nought, ha, ha!" The uncle realizes his slip, asks for for-
giveness, gets it, and leaves for home bouncing with happiness. Criseyde
moves into her closet, sits down "as stylle as any ston," turns all his
words over in her mind, is somewhat astonished "for the newe cas," but
when she fully considers it she finds she has no danger to fear. At this
point Chaucer gives us his and his heroine's explanation for Criseyde's
new peace of mind:

For man may love, of possibilite,
A womman so, his herte may tobreste,
And she naught love ayein, but if hire leste.

Now, this is clearly a key moment in Chaucer's understanding and presentation of Criseyde's character (the lines have no counterpart in the *Filostrato*). Criseyde has nothing to fear because she cannot be *forced* to love Troilus back. In fact, this is also Criseyde's and Chaucer's answer to Dante's Francesca. If I may formulate it in my own travesty of Dante's Italian: "Amore all'amato *puote* perdonare." Thus, Francesca's shadow seems to have disappeared. As if to confirm this, sixty lines later Chaucer feels the need to say in authorial or narratorial voice, and after one of the most enchanting, romantic scenes of the poem ("Who yaf me drynke?" readers will remember) that if envious people now started accusing Criseyde of loving Troilus "lightly" and "suddenly," "at first sight," he would feel obliged to reply that she did *not* "so sodeynly" give him her love but that she began to incline to like him first, and "after that" his manhood and his torments made love "mine" within her, breaking into her heart:

For which by proces and by good servyse
He gat hire love, and in no sodeyn wyse

Boccaccio's Criseida, by contrast, "sì *subitamente* presa fue, / che sopra ogni altro bene lui disia." In other words, as far as Criseyde is concerned, there is no love at first glance, no *coup-de-foudre*. "Amor al cor gentil ratto *non* s'apprende." Thus, Francesca's first law, her Guinizzellian misreading, goes to the dogs, too. With it, Francesca's misuse of "Andreas Capellanus" also disappears: as if denying one of the *De Amore*'s assumptions, Criseyde will later reject the proposition that "jalousie is love." Finally, the solitude of the two lovers decreases drastically (Troilus and Criseyde are practically never alone). And the book—that *Lancelot* which women, according to Chaucer's own Nun's Priest, hold "in full greet reverence"—is tantalizingly present in the consummation scene only as the reflex of a put-on appearance, when Pandarus finally withdraws to the fire, takes a light, and finds a "contenaunce, / As for to loke upon an old romaunce."

Criseyde is no Francesca (and no Paolo either, in spite of her initiative in kissing Troilus). This is one reason why Chaucer did not use

"Amor ch'al cor gentil ratto s'apprende" but Guinizzelli's "Al cor gentile rempaira sempre amore." He wished to take *two* hearts—both the man's and the woman's—into account. Thus, "in gentil hertes ay redy to repaire." In the plural, it could be predicated of both Troilus and Criseyde.

Yet this is only a part—and a minor one—of the answer to my initial question. In Chaucer's *Troilus*, Criseyde has a powerfully new feminine autonomy, but she is still the object of Troilus's love and of the narrator's writing. And, to begin with the latter, in his eyes Criseyde looks more like a Beatrice than a Francesca. The author offers us two portraits of his heroine, one at the beginning and one at the end of the poem. Both exalt her beauty, though the latter provides us with more details and with a slightly disturbing trait. In the former, Chaucer seems to go back to the analogy proposed by Guinizzelli in the last stanza of "Al cor gentile" as well as to Dante's frequent comparisons between Beatrice and an angel:

> Criseyde was this lady name al right.
> As to my doom, in al Troies cite
> Nas non so fair, forpassynge every wight,
> So aungelik was hir natif beaute,
> That lik a thing immortal semed she,
> As doth an hevenyssh perfit creature,
> That down were sent in scornynge of nature.

One could of course object that these were common conceits in all courtly love poetry so that there would be no need to find a source for this passage in Guinizzelli or Dante. But when the final portrait is presented, precisely mirroring the first so as to frame the entire poem, Chaucer's recourse to Dante cannot be denied. For this time he concentrates on Criseyde's eyes and, like Dante in "Amor che ne la mente mi ragiona," the *Convivio,* and *Paradiso* XVIII, he sees them as a mirror of Paradise:

> But for to speken of hire eyen cleere,
> Lo, trewely, they writen that hire syen
> That Paradis stood formed in hire yen.

The author, then, seems to understand Dante's sublimation discourse but interestingly refrains from allegorical interpretation, placing the burden of the analogy on those writers who have "seen" Criseyde (but which "writer" has ever seen her?). For Chaucer, Criseyde is a woman of flesh and blood, and indeed of soul and mind wonderfully feminine—*therefore* an angel, whose eyes reflect Paradise. She is the paradigm of human changeableness, yet her heavenly beauty shines, immovable, even beyond her "change"—even as she forsakes Troilus.

A fundamental transformation takes place in Troilus, too. The love which at first he experiences as an unbearable Petrarchan conflict of opposed feelings and physical sensations, as Keats's "mere commingling of passionate breath," he perceives—when reciprocal submission and union with the beloved are achieved—as an aspect of cosmic eros. The process begins in Troilus's famous hymn to Love-Charity halfway through Book III and culminates in his "Canticus" at the end of the same Book. It is a process rooted in physical pleasure—the "heaven" in which Troilus delights before pronouncing that hymn is Criseyde's body, which he caresses and kisses—but it is also capable of rising to the higher spheres of Venus and Hymen, of envisaging love as *caritas,* and of praising it as the "holy bond of thynges" with the words Dante's Saint Bernard had used of the Virgin in his prayer in *Paradiso* XXXIII:

> che qual vuol grazia e a te non ricorre
> sua disianza vuol volar sanz'ali
> Whoso wol grace and list the nought honouren,
> Lo, his desir wol fle withouten wynges.

Again, Troilus's Boethian "Canticus" at the end of Book III is inspired by Criseyde's "womanhede" and beauty. But once more, Troilus is able to join the earthly and cosmic sides of eros. In the song Chaucer rearranges metrum 7 of *Consolatio* II—a poem which celebrates the "amor quo caelum regitur"—so as to make it begin with the triple anaphora of "Love":

> Love, that of erthe and se hath governaunce,
> Love, that his hestes hath in hevene hye,
> Love, that with an holsom alliaunce

"Francesca's voice is only a whisper," Karla Taylor has beautifully said of this passage. That whisper seems about to become Dante's glorious proclamation of "l'amor che move il sole e l'altre stelle." Troilus does not make this final leap explicitly, yet does see God (who is absent in the Boethian source) as He who wills Love to "cerclen hertes alle and faste bynde" with its chain. The "auctour of kynde," the Creator of Nature, initiates the movement of Love that keeps the universe together. Troilus's most exalted, semiparadisal vision springs from a pan-erotic feeling inspired by love for a human being, by the happiness of returned eros on earth. Francesca may yet become Beatrice.

The narrator had anticipated this move in his own Prologue to Book III. There, Venus does not appear as the source of "folle amore" whom pagans, according to Dante's *Paradiso* VIII, believed her to be but rather as the Lucretian "voluptas" of men and gods, the blissful light of the third heaven (the very heaven of *Paradiso* VIII and of "Voi che intendendo il terzo ciel movete"), and the "plesance of love" "in gentil hertes ay redy to repaire." It is this double aspect of eros that Chaucer's choice of the Guinizzellian line signals. Love shines from the third heaven ("Splende 'n la 'ntelligenzia del cielo," Guinizzelli had written in his fifth stanza). That is its "kyndely stede" in the cosmos. From there, it is always ready to return to its mansion on earth, in the noble heart, and this movement is both constant and natural. More generally, the "vapour," the emanation through which the entire universe feels the power of love, is "eterne."

And now comes Chaucer's fundamental addition to his Boccaccian and Boethian sources: "God loveth, and to love wol nought werne." At the end of Book III, Troilus will see God as the initiator of love. Here, the author anticipates and complements that vision by looking at love as God's dominant characteristic. "Deus amat," "Deus est Amor": God is the subject, the object, and the ultimate "kyndely stede" of human and cosmic eros. "The sexual urge that is the subject of this stanza" thus becomes, as Peter Dronke writes, "a counterpart and reflection of the highest love. For a moment it is the Christian God partaking in his own loving creation."

In sum, Chaucer seems to understand the analogies of Guinizzelli's canzone and to interpret them as a sequence that sketches in a double— downward and upward—movement in a Dantean perspective. Francesca may yet lead to Beatrice. What is still missing from Chaucer's vision is what I have called the view of love from beyond death. Beautifully if obliquely, this emerges at the end of the poem, in the so-called Epilogue.

Here, Chaucer is quick to seize on the death of Troilus to leap, unlike the Boccaccio of the *Filostrato,* beyond it.

This journey to the other world is once more double. On the one hand, the soul of Troilus ascends, like that of Arcita in the *Teseida,* to the eighth sphere, contemplates the "pleyn felicite" of heaven, and, with "disembodied laughter," despises this wretched world, condemns the "blynde lust, the which that may nat laste," and is finally led by Mercury Psychopompos to an unknown destination. Two points are notable here. First, Troilus's soul is not condemned to the first circle of Hell where, pagan or no pagan, the Dantean Minos whom he had himself recalled earlier on would have destined him. Second, Troilus understands now, after death, that God, Whom he had seen as the initiator of love, should in turn be loved. Human "lust" is now called "blind" because it is short-lived, focussed only on a transient good, whereas we "sholden al our herte on heven caste"—direct our love to its eternal end and source. I would not call this a recantation but a deeper comprehension.

Troilus's vision after death offers the author the opportunity to complete his own discourse about love. He does this by using Troilus's experience in the other world, but going beyond it to return to earth and reestablish the double heaven-earth, earth-heaven movement. "God loveth," he had proclaimed in the prologue to Book III. He repeats it now, seeing Christ as he who "right for *love* / Upon a crois, oure soules for to beye, / First starf, and roos, and sit in hevene above"—in other words, placing at the centre of divine love that incarnation which made God suffer a *human* death in order to redeem mankind and then that resurrection which finally made the divinity return to its proper mansion in heaven. But he also widens the perspective by going back to God the Creator. When he addresses the "yonge, fresshe folkes," he is careful to add that in them love grows with their age, and after inviting them to "repeyre hom fro worldly vanite," he exhorts them to cast their hearts' eyes to that God who created them in his image, after his likeness. God loves, and his love is reflected, growing with age, in the heart of those creatures which resemble him. Human love and divine love can, however obliquely, meet. One is the image of the other. Hence, we must not forget that this world is like a fair and like the transient beauty of flowers but must appreciate it all the more since God himself created it and suffered death to redeem it.

Chaucer has grasped the meaning of Dante's great metamorphosis by following the movement of Guinizzelli's canzone beyond death and interpreting it with originality and complexity—by "improving" the invention—in the light of the *Divine Comedy*. It is significant that his final prayer in the *Troilus* should be addressed to the Trinity and in particular to the love which its second, incarnated person, Jesus, bore to his Virgin Mother. The first three lines of this prayer are directly translated from the song of praise pronounced by the spirits of the "sapientes" in Dante's Heaven of the Sun (*Paradiso* XIV):

> Thow oon, and two, and thre, eterne on lyve,
> That regnest ay in thre, and two, and oon,
> Uncircumscript, and al maist circumscrive

> Quell'uno e due e tre che sempre vive
> e regna sempre in tre e 'n due e 'n uno,
> non circunscritto, e tutto circunscrive

When the chant is over, one of the spirits, Solomon, explains to Dante how the light that enfolds each soul—a light which shines brightly and constantly because it is the manifestation of the blessed soul's *love* for God—will become infinitely greater after the resurrection, when the flesh shall "dress" the soul again. Solomon's fervid speech prompts such an immediate and eager "Amen" from the other spirits that Dante understands how great their desire must be for their dead bodies. As in the Song of Songs, which the Middle Ages attributed to Solomon, divine love and human love are celebrated together. When Dante adds with an extraordinary touch that the "sapientes" yearn for their body "forse non pur per lor, ma per le mamme, / per li padri e per li altri che fuor cari / anzi che fosser sempiterne fiamme" (not so much for themselves, but perhaps for their mothers, their fathers, and all those who were dear to them before they became sempiternal flames), *we* understand why Chaucer chose those three lines to conclude *Troilus and Criseyde*. Now, from beyond death, he could fully see why this life is so important. Now, from beyond the Heaven of Venus, he could propose his own vision—a vision I would call, not, as C. S. Lewis did, the "Allegory," but the *Analogy* of Love.

The love we feel on earth for another human being—Troilus's physical and courtly love for Criseyde—makes us feel the love by which the cosmos is ruled. Apparently, we cannot go beyond this analogy. Yet, as the prologue to Book III indicates and as Troilus himself feels at the end of that Book, universal eros appertains to and is initiated by God. And divine love is in turn, as the Epilogue suggests, mirrored in man. This final analogy we can only perceive if we look at things with eyes that have experienced death, when our soul—as in Guinizzelli's canzone—faces the Absolute. From there, we may see medieval love poetry as one step in the complex analogical chain which constitutes the human discourse about desire and love: in Keatsian terms, how flowers would not bloom, fruit would not swell to melting pulp, fish would not have bright mail, and the earth its dower of river, wood, and vale, if human souls did never kiss and greet (*Endymion* I, 835–42). From there, in short, we can fully comprehend why the blissful light that adorneth all the third heaven fair is "in *our* gentil hertes ay redy to repaire."

CHAPTER THREE

The Genius to Improve an Invention

Transformations of the Knight's Tale

In the long preface to the *Fables,* Dryden not only compares the authors of the stories he translates for the collection but also discusses their sources. What he says about the first of the tales is very interesting in this respect. After giving the "Noble Poem" of Palamon and Arcite an epic status "perhaps not much inferiour" to that of the *Iliad* and the *Aeneid,* Dryden maintains that he had thought this story to be "of *English* Growth, and *Chaucer's* own." But, he adds,

> I was undeceiv'd by *Boccace;* for casually looking on the End of his seventh Giornata, I found *Dioneo* (under which name he shadows himself) and *Fiammetta* (who represents his Mistress, the natural Daughter of *Robert* King of *Naples*) of whom these words are spoken. *Dioneo e Fiammetta gran pezza cantarono insieme d'Arcita, e di Palamone;* by which it appears that this Story was written before the time of *Boccace;* but the name of its Author being wholly lost, *Chaucer* is now become an Original; and I question not but the Poem has receiv'd many Beauties by passing through his Noble Hands.

It is rather strange that, having made the connection between Boccaccio, the author of the *Decameron,* and Dioneo, one of the characters in the *Decameron's* frame, who is said to have "sung" of Arcite and Palamon,

Dryden should not suspect that the story had been first written by Boccaccio himself (in the *Teseida*). But the most important aspect of Dryden's source hunting in the preface is not philological accuracy: it is,
rather, an attitude toward his poetic forebears which reveals a good deal
about Dryden's own approach to the *Fables*. In these, he mostly translates or adopts stories written by Homer, Ovid, Boccaccio, and Chaucer. The general problem of "borrowing" preexisting material becomes,
therefore, a personal one, and Dryden sublimates any "anxiety of influence" from which he may suffer by inserting himself into the universal
pattern of literary imitation. Neither Ovid nor Chaucer, he declares, were
great inventors, the former having only "copied the *Grecian* Fables," the
latter having taken most of his stories "from his Italian Contemporaries,
or their Predecessors." Furthermore, Dryden significantly extends his
considerations on the practice of "translation" or "adaptation" to the
whole of English culture, thus implicitly shifting the focus to make room
for himself: "the Genius of our Countrymen in general" is, he writes,
"rather to improve an Invention, than to invent themselves; as is evi-
dent not only in our Poetry, but in many of our Manufactures."

As a generalization, this statement hardly holds water. Where would
one, in such a context, place Shakespeare, Newton, or Dickens? However, my intention in this chapter is to see whether that generalization
applies to the particular chain of literary works which stem from Chaucer's *Knight's Tale*, *The Two Noble Kinsmen* of Shakespeare and Fletcher,
and Dryden's own *Palamon and Arcite*.

The story of Palamon and Arcite has at least two features in common
with that of Troilus and Cressida which I have examined in the preceding chapter. The first is an aspect of the history of European literature and hence of the European imagination: this is their passing from
the hands of Boccaccio to those of Chaucer, Shakespeare, and Dryden.
The second may be one of the reasons for their extraordinary success,
and this is that at the centre of both stand two men and a woman. In the
Troilus and Cressida plot we are presented with a version of the love tri-
angle that ends up in betrayal on the part of the lady—a variation of
the adultery pattern which is common in Western literature since its very
beginning. In the Palamon and Arcite story we find a version of an archetypal moment of animal life: the fight of two males for the same female.
Arcite and Palamon, the two noble Thebans Theseus captures after sack-
ing Thebes, fall in love, by looking outside of their Athenian prison onto

the palace garden, with the young sister-in-law, Emily, of the "Duke" of Athens and end up by fighting a duel. Surprised by Theseus, they are forced to fight in a true tourney, the winner of which will obtain the lady. Before the tournament, the two lovers pray to the gods: Arcite invokes Mars and asks for victory; Palamon addresses Venus and asks for Emily. The gods turn to Saturn to solve the problem. And the solution is that Arcite, who wins the tourney, falls from his horse, frightened by the sudden appearance of a Fury evoked by Saturn, and dies. Palamon marries Emily.

Violent animal imagery characterizes both Chaucer's *Knight's Tale* and Dryden's *Palamon and Arcite,* and it also surfaces in *The Two Noble Kinsmen.* The martial Muse, whether in romance, epic, or drama, is of course fond of lions, tigers, bears, and boar, and in his attempt at re-creating classical epos in the *Teseida* Boccaccio uses similes that go back, through Statius's *Thebaid,* to Virgil's *Aeneid* and ultimately to Homer's *Iliad.* By concentrating such imagery into very dense clusters, Chaucer reveals that he is not merely imitating the epic style but in fact introducing into the story an elemental, instinctual fury absent in his source. The scene in which the two lovers meet for their duel in the grove is a characteristic instance of this. They are first compared to hunters waiting for the lion or the bear; then, when the fight begins, the hunters become animals, and three similes are piled upon each other in quick succession:

> Thou myghtest wene that this Palamon
> In his fighting were a wood leon,
> And as a cruel tigre was Arcite;
> As wilde bores gone they to smyte,
> That frothen whit as foom for ire wood.

Fletcher, who is responsible for the corresponding scene of *The Two Noble Kinsmen,* drops this kind of imagery, not essential on a stage where two actors can shout at each other and effectively mimic their "ire" by brandishing swords. But a bear simile is used by Shakespeare during Arcite's and Palamon's first encounter, and Theseus likens them to "a pair of lions, smeared with prey" when, in Shakespeare's first act, he recalls their fighting in the battle over Thebes.

Shakespeare and Fletcher, however, as we shall later see, are interested in different animal correlatives. Dryden, on the other hand, keeps

Chaucer's images and indeed "fortifies" them according to his conception of an epic poem (the only defect he sees in Chaucer is the diction, the "Words," because, coming "in the Dawning of our Language," Chaucer "wanted the "Modern Art of Fortifying"), but he also "improves" Boccaccio's and Chaucer's "inventions" by catching precisely the archetypal meaning of the scene. His two boars do not merely, like Chaucer's, foam at the mouth "for ire wood"; they show us their bristles and their tusks and make us hear their grunts and groans. In short, his Palamon and Arcite are really animal-like, and Dryden in fact adds an apparently superfluous detail which however reveals to us that he has fully understood the issue: two males are fighting for a female, and the cause is love:

> Fell *Arcite* like an angry Tyger far'd,
> And like a Lion *Palamon* appear'd:
> Or as two Boars whom Love to Battle draws,
> With rising Bristles, and with froathy Jaws,
> Their adverse Breasts with Tusks oblique they wound;
> With Grunts and Groans the Forest rings around.

Later in *Palamon and Arcite* Dryden shows himself much more aware of this element than Chaucer. In describing the paintings in the temple of Venus, he mentions, following the *Knight's Tale,* "Medea's Charms" and "Circean Feasts." Again, he adds a line which at first sight looks like a mere decorative filler or a pompous classical allusion but which on a second reading points to deeper and wider implications: "*Circean* Feasts, / With Bowls that turn'd inamour's Youth to Beasts." Thus, one of Dryden's "improvements" consists in his making explicit a central theme of Chaucer's *Tale*—the contrast and complementarity of animal and human that the contest between Palamon and Arcite implies.

In Chaucer, *eros* inflames the two lovers transforming them, as Dryden makes clear, into brutes. But in reading the *Knight's Tale* we also become aware that it is *eros* which turns both heroes into thinking human beings. Before falling in love, Chaucer's Palamon and Arcite dwell in the tower "in angwissh and in wo"; after seeing Emily, they start arguing with logic if not with actual sophistry. Soon after, they become philosophers expounding at length their views of the human condition. Dryden keeps this feature of Chaucer's story. Shakespeare eliminates all philosophical considerations but, as we shall presently see, highlights the contrast by underlining with greater emphasis than either his predecessor or his successor an opposition that lies at the heart of the story, that between *philia* and *eros.*

From the very beginning in Boccaccio's *Teseida* an essential feature of the Palamon and Arcite plot is not only their contending for the same lady but also their being "noble," "of royal blood," and "parenti," relatives. With Chaucer, this feature is made more prominent through repetition of words like "cosyn," but Shakespeare and Fletcher place it at the very centre of their play, which is significantly titled "The Two *Noble Kinsmen.*" Thus, an opposition between "nobility" and the basic human drive of possession in love—between courtliness and instinct, ultimately between culture and nature—is added to that between *philia* and *eros.* In turn, *philia* means both "friendship" and "kinship." Our authors seem to be aware of the potentialities which this wide spectrum of contrasts opens up. The teller of the *Knight's Tale,* for instance, interprets the *philia/eros* dichotomy as one between Cupid and "charity," between "love" and "felaweshipe." In this, he is followed by Dryden:

> O Cupide, out of alle charitee!
> O regne, that wolt no felawe have with thee!
> Ful sooth is seyd that love ne lordshipe
> Wol noght, his thankes, have no felaweshipe.

> Oh Love! Thou sternly dost thy Pow'r maintain,
> And wilt not bear a Rival in thy Reign,
> Tyrants and thou all Fellowship disdain.

But Dryden emphasizes the friendship element much more than Chaucer. Thus, when Arcite answers Palamon's argument on the "Eldership of Right" with his "no Law is made for Love," Dryden fills out the original, "improving" it:

> If then the Laws of Friendship I transgress,
> I keep the Greater, while I break the less.

At the end of the same scene he adds several lines that have no precedent in Chaucer's *Tale.* Here, he underlines the turning of friendship into hate, with vivid visual touches and the inevitable insertion of the animal correlative:

> Great was their Strife, which hourly was renew'd,
> Till each with mortal Hate his Rival view'd:
> Now Friends no more, nor walking Hand in Hand;
> But when they met, they made a surly Stand;
> And glar'd like angry Lions as they pass'd,
> And wish'd that ev'ry Look might be their last.

Shakespeare and Fletcher, however, are much more radical in their exploitation of such contrasts. They expand the *philia/eros* opposition at both ends and give a completely new turn to the instinctual/courtly dichotomy by introducing the subplot of the Gaoler's daughter's love for Palamon.

That Theseus and Perotheus love each other "tendrely" we know already from the *Knight's Tale* and indeed from classical tradition and Boccaccio's *Teseida*. But Shakespeare's Hippolyta (the wife Theseus has conquered by defeating the Amazons, whose queen she was) describes this "friendship" to Emilia in terms that go far beyond any Chaucer could conceive, as far in fact as to maintain that Theseus would be unable to choose between love for his wife and love for his friend:

> Their knot of love,
> Tied, weaved, entangled, with so true, so long,
> And with a finger of so deep a cunning,
> May be outworn, never undone. I think
> Theseus cannot be umpire to himself,
> Cleaving his conscience into twain and doing
> Each side like justice, which he loves best.

Shakespeare makes the theme much more relevant by adding a wholly new "invention." Immediately after Hippolyta's statement, Emilia recalls her onetime playfellow Flavina. Pirithous's and Theseus's love, she says, "has more ground, is more maturely seasoned, / More buckled with strong judgement, and their needs / The one of th'other may be said to water / Their intertangled roots of love." She and Flavina, then both eleven years old, loved each other in total innocence, simply because they did, with no ulterior motive. The relationship between the two girls represents *philia* in all its complexity, in its primal child- and adolescent-like, purely homosexual quality. Indeed, it is opposed, and considered as superior to, love between different sexes: "the true love 'tween maid and maid may be / More than in sex dividual."

Not content with this, Shakespeare transforms the Arcite-Palamon relationship into one in which *philia* appears much more prominent and complex than in Chaucer. When we first see the two characters, Theseus's attack on Thebes is being launched. Arcite invites Palamon, "dearer in love than blood," to leave the city and the vices of Creon's court. The *philia* between them is tinged with a Stoical, almost Brutus-like disdain for corruption and tyranny and with a patriotic, almost nineteenth-century response to the call of king and country. The next time we see them, in the Athenian jail, all that is left to them is precisely their friendship. Thebes, friends, kindred, "games of honour" are gone. They are prisoners, they think, forever, and in prison their youth "must wither / Like a too timely spring." Furthermore, they can entertain no hope of ever acquiring "a loving wife," of knowing "issue," of ever seeing "figures of [themselves] to glad [their] age." As Arcite puts it,

> This is all our world;
> We shall know nothing here but one another,
> Hear nothing but the clock that tells our woes.

Philia becomes an existential necessity as well as a philosophical choice and a kind of protohomosexual love:

> From all that fortune can inflict upon us,
> I see two conforts rising, two mere blessings,
> If the gods please; to hold here a brave patience,
> And the enjoying of our griefs together.
> [. . .]
> And here being thus together,
> We are an endless mine to one another;
> We are one another's wife, ever begetting
> New births of love; we are father, friends, acquaintance;
> We are, in one another, families.

From this we pass, in the same scene, to the harsh quarrel between Arcite and Palamon after they see Emilia. The tragic irony of their *philia* is fully exposed by the raging of *eros*.

Lest we forget that this is the central theme of the play, Shakespeare now indirectly extends it to Emilia, who, in gathering flowers in the garden, picks a narcissus and exclaims, "That was a fair boy, certain, but a fool / To love himself; were there not maids enough?" only to conclude: "Men are mad things." Two acts later, she has changed her mind. Fletcher seizes on Shakespeare's image with the gusto one would expect of the author of most of the Gaoler's Daughter's subplot. Emilia is comparing her two lovers: she extols Arcite and despises Palamon, "a mere dull shadow" to his cousin. She singles out all the defects of Palamon's appearance and character, but, suddenly, she sees them in a new light:

Yet these that we count errors may become him;
Narcissus was a sad boy, but a heavenly.
O, who can find the bent of a woman's fancy?
I am a fool; my reason is lost in me,
I have no choice, and I have lied so lewdly
That women ought to beat me.

Eros has conquered her, too; she is uncertain between Palamon and Arcite, but her "fancy" now cries for both lovers.

Emilia—the difference from Chaucer is quite remarkable—proclaims herself a fool. But the Gaoler's Daughter becomes, in the words of one of the peasants, "as mad as a March hare." The animal image stands at the very centre of the play. The epic context, however, has been completely eliminated and replaced by popular, proverbial wisdom pointing to starkly naked eros if not to actual lechery.

The subplot of the Gaoler's Daughter occupies nine scenes from the second to the fifth Act of The Two Noble Kinsmen. There is no room here to illustrate in detail its furious, spectacular crescendo, but it is important to point out its most significant stages in order to understand how Shakespeare and Fletcher have altered Chaucer's romance. Already in the first scene of Act II the Gaoler's Daughter shows herself to be the opposite of Emilia. Emilia will never really manage to choose between Arcite and Palamon; the Gaoler's Daughter immediately distinguishes between them and interestingly enough points to Palamon. Two scenes later, the girl is already lost. Aware of the social difference between her and Palamon, that "to marry him is hopeless; / To be his whore is witless," she however deludes herself into thinking that once she frees him

from prison he shall love her. She reconstructs with obsessive precision
the stages of her falling in love with him: first came sight, then appreci-
ation, then pity, finally love—an "extreme" and "infinite" love which she
herself shortly afterward considers as "beyond love, and beyond reason, /
Or wit, or safety." In the fifth scene of Act II, although she is conscious
of the fact that Palamon has paid her no attention, the girl fosters her
illusion and mentally abandons herself to him:

> Let him do
> What he will with me, so he use me kindly;
> For use me so he shall, or I'll proclaim him,
> And to his face, no man . . .

The monologue from which these lines are taken closes Act II. Act III
opens with the famous monologue in which Arcite sings his great hymn
of love for Emilia, "jewel o' th'wood, o' th'world," who has "blessed a
place" with her "sole presence." The two scenes are thus deliberately set
in ironical contrast to each other: pure, exalted, courtly, male love against
direct, improper, violent female *eros*. In the third Act, the latter's progress
toward madness is inexorable. The girl is at first suspended between, on
the one hand, the construction of a fictional reality to fence off the realization that Palamon does not care for her and, on the other, the recognition that this is a "lie," that "the best way is the next way to the grave, /
Each errant step beside is torment." Finally, she plunges into the storm.
The sea images recall those of Shakespeare's later plays (*Pericles, The Tempest, The Winter's Tale*), but in fact Fletcher goes back to the "tempest" in
Lear's mind.

After seeing her join the Schoolmaster and the peasants for the mor-
ris dance in III, v, we find the Gaoler's Daughter again at the beginning
of Act IV. Her Wooer describes her here as a sort of Pyramus looking for
his Thisbe-Palamon ("gone to th'wood to gather mulberries"), but also
as an Ophelia:

> her careless tresses
> A wreath of bulrush rounded; about her stuck
> Thousand of fresh flowers of several colours,
> That methought she appeared like a fair nymph
> That feeds the lake with waters

The topic of all her speeches when she appears again on the stage is, quite openly, her desire ("I must lose my maidenhead by cocklight"), which she cries out roaringly, drowning all sounds of martial combat, precisely when, with another proverbial animal image, she announces her silence: "yet I keep close for all this, / Close as a cockle."

The culminating point of the subplot is, however, that which apparently brings it to its dénouement—the moment when the fiction invented by the Doctor and played out by the Wooer "cures" the girl. For the Gaoler's Daughter really seems to believe that the man who stands before her and courts her is Palamon, but a few minutes later seems to think that Palamon is far away, so that we have no way of determining whether she has accepted this fiction unconsciously or willingly. Thus, we perceive the last lines of the scene as a moment of supreme pathos: when, whatever his identity may be, she takes the Wooer as a *man* who will finally satisfy her desire without hurting her:

> DAUGHTER: And then we'll sleep together.
> DOCTOR: Take her offer.
> WOOER: Yes, marry, will we.
> DAUGHTER: But you shall not hurt me.
> WOOER: I will not, sweet.
> DAUGHTER: If you do, love, I'll cry.

Shakespeare and Fletcher have then transformed the very coordinates of the story. While, following Chaucer, they show us two men in love with a woman, they add a woman in love with a man. The passion of the Gaoler's Daughter, the only functional motivation for which in the play is that of being instrumental to Palamon's liberation, constitutes a central ploy of *The Two Noble Kinsmen*. This is a passion that belongs to the lower classes, and its explicitly sexual bent and violence highlight with dramatic irony what lies behind the apparently courtly contest of Palamon and Arcite. Thus, the contrast between the courtly and the instinctual, the cultural and the natural, is transposed onto a social plane (aristocracy vs. lower classes), but also, by its being extended to yet another realm of society, increased in intensity.

The role of the Gaoler's Daughter's plot is, however, more complex. The story of Palamon and Arcite traditionally presents us with a powerful image of male desire. The Gaoler's Daughter forcefully asserts the existence of woman's desire. If the former leads to a relentless struggle the final outcome of which is the death of one of the two suitors (*eros* gives way to *thanatos*), the latter leads to total madness. The two kinds of violence are presented as parallel and equally extreme, but there is a fundamental difference between them. Palamon's and Arcite's love for Emilia becomes a cosmic conflict, one between transhuman powers such as Venus and Mars, and its solution lies, as Theseus proclaims at the end of the play, with fortune and the gods. The Gaoler's Daughter's love is never reciprocated and arouses an exclusively inner conflict. In *The Two Noble Kinsmen* the wholly external violence of the contest between the two lovers becomes unbearable because it finds a counterpart in something that comes to divide the mind itself of a human being. The Gaoler's Daughter pays for her love with her own soul.

Finally, the solution is, in her case, wholly human. Neither fate nor the gods have anything to do with it. Like Arcite's in the *Knight's Tale*, here is a "maladye / Of Hereos" and a "manye, / Engendred of humour melancolik," and as such it is dealt with by a physician who shows himself to be both sensible and radical, a genius of diagnosis as well as in stage directing: if necessary, passion is treated by fiction, "a falsehood with falsehoods combated"; in any case it will be cured by sex. And while Arcite must die so that Palamon, who was first in seeing Emily, can enjoy his "right," the Gaoler's Daughter's Wooer must pretend to be Palamon and promise to make love to her in order to cure her. In other words, this time the male must die to himself, give up his identity and at the same time satisfy his desire in order to help and love the woman.

Shakespeare and Fletcher have, then, not just "improved" an "invention." They have radically revolutionized the story, and perhaps their "anxiety of influence" toward Chaucer should not be seen as a purely rhetorical stance even though it shows itself to be a "fear" soon overcome rather than the typically Oedipal anguish Harold Bloom thinks of. Chaucer's *Tale*, the prologue proclaims, represents an ideal, changeless, eternal model; yet Chaucer himself is dead and buried, and his rattling bones, his words coming out of the grave, must make a spectator smile:

Chaucer, of all admired, the story gives;
There constant to eternity it lives.
If we let fall the nobleness of this,
And the first sound this child hear be a hiss,

How will it shake the bones of that good man,
And make him cry from under ground "O, fan
From me the witless chaff of such a writer
That blasts my bays and my famed works makes lighter
Than Robin Hood!" This is the fear we bring;
For, to say the truth, it were an endless thing,
And too ambitious, to aspire to him.

Having set aside any aspiration and ambition to fight against their father, Shakespeare and Fletcher then proceed to change the conception itself of love as a force that presides over or determines the fates of their characters. Thus, for instance, the prayer of Chaucer's Palamon to Venus is a speech full of contrasts between light and dark, positive and negative. In it, the might of the goddess is exalted, but the emphasis is, throughout, on old age, and the result is that what impresses us is not the power of love but a series of images of decay. The development of the love theme in *The Two Noble Kinsmen* is, as we have seen, a completely different business.

Dryden, who does not hesitate to stress the violence implicit in Palamon's and Arcite's contest for Emily, considers love as such in a wholly favourable way, celebrating Venus as creator in an enthusiastically Lucretian, Chaucerian, and Spenserian hymn. Before this Venus even the lion "loaths the Taste of Blood," and the male's hunt for the female becomes a perfectly natural, even playful occupation (the opposite of what is happening in the story at this point and of what earlier animal imagery had suggested):

Creator *Venus*, Genial Pow'r of Love,
The Bliss of Men below, and Gods above,
Beneath the sliding Sun thou runn'st thy Race,
Dost fairest shine, and best become thy Place.
For thee the Winds their Eastern Blasts forbear,
Thy Month reveals the Spring, and opens all the Year.
Thee, Goddess, thee the Storms of Winter fly,
Earth smiles with Flow'rs renewing; laughs the Sky,
And Birds to Lays of Love their tuneful Notes apply.
For thee the Lion loaths the Taste of Blood,
And roaring hunts his Female through the Wood:

For thee the Bulls rebellow trough the Groves,
And tempt the Stream, and snuff their absent Loves.
'Tis thine, whate'er is pleasant, good, or fair:
All Nature is thy Province, Life thy Care;
Thou mad'st the World, and dost the World repair.

The contrast between Mars and Venus is an integral part of the story ever since Boccaccio's *Teseida*. When Venus herself turns into an ambiguous entity, the conflict between the two divinities becomes less explicit. Individual godheads occupy a far less prominent place in *The Two Noble Kinsmen* than in the *Knight's Tale*: their temples, their quarrel, the intervention of Jupiter and Saturn disappear. In Chaucer, Arcite's fatal accident is a result of Saturn's direct action: the god asks Pluto to send an infernal Fury to startle the hero's horse. Shakespeare attributes the event to natural causes, endowing them with saturnine qualities but refraining from decisively committing himself to the involvement of supernatural powers:

what envious flint,
Cold as old Saturn and like him possessed
With fire malevolent, darted a spark,
Or what fierce sulphur else, to this end made,
I comment not.

What becomes ever more oppressive in *The Two Noble Kinsmen*, particularly toward the end of the play, is the dark presence of indeterminate divine entities, indicated simply as the "heavenly powers" or the "gods." Theseus alone returns—and briefly at that—to the logic of his Chaucerian predecessor when, after Arcite's death, he offers Palamon an explanation that points to Venus and Mars as to the single gods that have dictated what he calls "due justice." When Palamon replies with a statement about the inherently tragic condition of man, who always loses what he most seeks, Theseus responds with a speech in which Fortune's paradoxical action and the gods' profound justice are opposed to each other and at the same time seen as complementary:

Never fortune
Did play a subtler game: the conquered triumphs,

The victor has the loss: *yet* in the passage
The gods have been most equal
[. . .]
The gods my justice
Take from my land, and they themselves become
The executioners.

Yet the conclusion of Theseus's speech—and of the play which ends with
it—is much more problematic. For meditating now on his own response
to the singular fate of Arcite and Palamon, the Duke of Athens seems to
question divine justice. With an image that recalls *King Lear,* he proclaims that human beings are "children" and the gods "charmers." While
the human condition is "baffling," the gods are mere enchanters, magi-
cians, illusion makers, tricksters. Thus, acceptance of "that which is"
means simply that the "dispute" between men and gods is only suspended, that the deeply, essentially human "question" is and will always
be asked, is and will always be unanswered by the gods:

        O you heavenly charmers,
    What things you make of us! For what we lack
    We laugh; for what we have are sorry; still
    Are children in some kind. Let us be thankful
    For that which is, and with you leave dispute
    That are above our question. Let's go off,
    And bear us like the time.

Nothing is more unlike this than the conclusion of Theseus's speech in
the *Knight's Tale:*

    What may I conclude of this longe serye,
    But after wo I rede us to be merye
    And thanken Jupiter of al this grace?

Shakespeare and Fletcher have "perverted" their Chaucer. On the other
hand, Dryden not only accepts fully the logic of Chaucer's Theseus, but
even "improves" on it by adding to his speech a whole new section on
the formation, development, and death of man that makes the argument
more cogent. Above all, he subtly modifies some details in the latter part

of the tale so as to prepare the ground for a less traumatic ending. For example, Dryden's dying Arcite is as sad and pessimistic as Chaucer's in seeing men "Now warm in Love, now with'ring in the Grave," but when he bequeaths the "service of his ghost" to Emily, he adds an apparently gratuitous touch of pathos:

> But to your Service I bequeath my Ghost;
> Which from this mortal Body when unty'd,
> Unseen, unheard, shall hover at your Side;
> Nor fright you waking, nor your Sleep offend,
> But wait officious, and your Steps attend.

In fact, this anticipates the position Dryden takes on the fate of Arcite's soul after death. At first sight, he seems here to agree with Chaucer's Knight (who had already turned upside down Boccaccio's story, in *Teseida* XI, of Arcite's ascent to the eighth sphere, which Chaucer instead adopts, as we have seen in chapter 2, for Troilus). "But whither went his Soul," Dryden writes, "let such relate / Who search the Secrets of the future State." Immediately afterward, however, he changes the approach. What becomes central is the insistence on the "strong proofs," the belief that if there were no mystery faith would no longer count:

> Strong Proofs they have, but not demonstrative:
> For, were all plain, then all Sides must agree,
> And Faith itself be lost in Certainty.

Dryden then appends a moral which has no antecedent in Chaucer and finally spells out the theologically (and culturally) correct destination of Arcite's soul—precisely the opposite of what the Knight would wish to do:

> To live uprightly then is sure the best,
> To save our selves, and not to damn the rest,
> The Soul of *Arcite* went, where Heathens go,
> Who better live than we, though less they know.

In other words, in Dryden an urge for consolation precedes the final recomposition of harmony such as we find in Chaucer. In the *Knight's*

Tale consolation is the job of Egeus, who knows "this worldes trans-mutacioun" and can therefore make gradual the passage from Arcite's death to Theseus's later philosophical (and political) solution: the harmony of the great chain of love willed by God and the marriage of Palamon and Emily. Dryden seizes on Egeus's speech but adds two lines that have no counterpart in the original: "With equal Mind, what happens, let us bear, / Nor joy, nor grieve too much for Things beyond our Care."

Here Shakespeare's Theseus would stop. But in Dryden's *Palamon and Arcite* these words represent only a first stage in the direction of final bliss. Thus prepared, the conclusion of Dryden's "fable" becomes a true neoclassical triumph such as Boccaccio may have dreamt of. In Palamon's prayer to Venus, Earth had smiled and the Sky had laughed to celebrate the goddess. Now, Venus herself smiles over Palamon. But, even more significantly, Eros and Anteros inflame bride and bridegroom during their "sweet laborious Night." Eros and Anteros are the sons that *Mars* (Mars, Venus's enemy in the story) has begotten by *Venus!* In Dryden's "improvement" of Chaucer's *Knight's Tale* the harmony now and forever reigning between Palamon and Emily corresponds to total peace in heaven. Without suffering any anxiety, Dryden has negotiated a compromise with his predecessor: unlike Shakespeare and Fletcher, he has taken away from his text all scepticism and all uncertainty, making fully explicit what his "father" had only suggested and, wherever necessary, subtly modifying (he would say, "fortifying") the original to adapt it to his needs. This, precisely, is "the genius to improve an invention."

CHAPTER FOUR

Are you here?

Brunetto, Dante, and Eliot

In this chapter I would like to explore the nature of the well-known relationship between two great masters of poetry, Dante and T. S. Eliot. The encounter between these two creators across the centuries is simply extraordinary, and although it has been the subject of innumerable essays in the past—indeed one of the two poets themselves, Eliot, often wrote about it—I still think it deserves further analysis and, what is more important, pure enjoyment.

I shall not speak about this relationship in general but will rather choose one particular instance of it, a famous one at that. The text we are starting from is section 2 of part II of *Little Gidding*, itself the fourth and last of Eliot's *Four Quartets*. The lines, "In the uncertain hour before the morning / Near the ending of interminable night," open a passage which describes the meeting between the poetic persona of the *Four Quartets* and the ghost "of some dead master" in the streets of London after an air raid during World War II. A short conversation between the two ensues, in the course of which the ghost speaks about poetry, time, and "the gifts reserved for age."

It has long been recognized—and Eliot himself made no mystery about it—that the inspiration behind this episode is fundamentally Dantean and that the source for it is principally canto XV of the *Inferno*, where the protagonist of the *Divine Comedy* meets his old master, Brunetto Latini: a scene which, Eliot tells us in his 1929 essay on Dante, impressed him at first reading and remained in his memory forever.

I shall soon return to *Inferno* XV. But first we must place the whole question of the relationship in its context; and here, too, Eliot himself helps us. In a memorable talk he gave in 1950 at the Italian Institute in London, "What Dante Means to Me," he spoke about *Little Gidding*:

> Twenty years after writing *The Waste Land*, I wrote, in *Little Gidding*, a passage which is intended to be the nearest equivalent to a canto of the Inferno or the Purgatorio, in style as well as content, that I could achieve. The intention, of course, was the same as with my allusions to Dante in *The Waste Land*: to present to the mind of the reader a parallel, by means of contrast, between the Inferno and the Purgatorio, which Dante visited and a hallucinated scene after an air-raid. But the method is different: here I was debarred from quoting or adapting at length—I borrowed and adapted freely only a few phrases—because I was *imitating*. My first problem was to find an approximation to the *terza rima* without rhyming.

Eliot went on to talk of Dante's verse and the problems which arise when one tries to translate or adapt it into English and concluded by saying that "This section of a poem—not the length of one canto of the Divine Comedy—cost [him] far more time and trouble and vexation than any passage of the same length that [he had] ever written."

Here, I would like to draw attention to three main points. First, Eliot himself indicates two aspects inherent in his imitation of Dante—one of style and one of content. Second, he tells us the method he adopted in following Dante: "to present to the mind of the reader *a parallel, by means of contrast*," between a Dantean scene and a contemporary one. Third, he mentions both *Inferno* and *Purgatorio*, does not refer to Brunetto in *Inferno* XV, and omits any reference to the *Paradiso*. It is on these three points that I shall concentrate.

If we turn to the manuscript draft of *Little Gidding* now in Magdalene College, Cambridge, we begin to understand the last two points I have mentioned and the link that connects them at a deep level. In the prose outline of the poem, Eliot's jottings point to the first movement of *Little Gidding* (without ever mentioning this name), in which against "midwinter spring" is set May time, and then to the second, the lyric piece where the death of air, earth, water and fire is described, in the following manner:

Winter scene. May.
Lyric. Air earth water end &
Daemonic fire. The inferno.

So far, fire is "daemonic" and the notes early allude to Hell as an image
of the modern city—an icon already found in *The Waste Land*—and to
Dante's *Inferno*. We might think we are back to that poem, where

A crowd flowed over London Bridge, so many,
I had not thought death hath undone so many.

Yet the second cluster of notes in the manuscipt draft seems to move in
an altogether different direction:

They vanish, the individuals, and our feeling for them sinks into the
flame which refines. They emerge in another pattern and recreated
and redeemed, reconciled, having their meaning together not apart
in a unison which is of beams from the central fire. And the others
with them contemporaneous. Invocation to the Holy Spirit.

In Dantean terms this is a movement through Purgatory up into Paradise. The first line of this note is indeed a fusion and an adaptation of
two lines from *Purgatorio* XXVI, in the first of which the father of Dolce
Stil Nuovo poetry, Guido Guinizzelli, "vanishes through fire" "come per
l'acqua il pesce andando al fondo"—as the fish does through water,
going to the bottom—whereas in the second the Provençal troubadour
Arnaut Daniel "s'ascose nel foco che gli affina," hides in the fire which
refines them. This, it will be remembered, is one of the "fragments" the
poetic persona of *The Waste Land* "shored against [his] ruins" at the very
end of that poem, before invoking "Shantih shantih shantih." Fire is no
longer "daemonic" but purgatorial. Immediately afterward, it becomes
pentecostal and heavenly: it is the fire of the third circle of Dante's final
vision of God in *Paradiso* XXXIII, the "foco che quinci e quindi igual-
mente si spiri" of the Holy Ghost. It is the fire that dominates the fourth
and fifth movements of *Little Gidding,* culminating in its union with
the rose.

In other words, the manuscript draft shows that *Little Gidding* is a
concentrated *Divine Comedy* which passes from *Inferno* to *Purgatorio* and

finally to *Paradiso*. This is made clear in lines 49–51 of the first movement, where the poet points to prayer and then announces a central Dantean message:

> And what the dead had no speech for, when living,
> They can tell you, being dead: the communication
> Of the dead is tongued with fire beyond the language of the living.

The journey to the other world is presented by Dante as the gradual revelation of truth by means of conversations with the souls of the damned, the penitent, and the blessed, and indeed as a passing "all'etterno dal tempo," from time to eternity—a central theme of the *Four Quartets*.

It is a meeting and a conversation with the "dead master" that dominates the second movement of *Little Gidding*. This is, then, the nearest that Eliot ever wrote not of a single scene but of the whole mechanism of the *Divine Comedy*. And that Dante's entire poem constitutes the background against which *Little Gidding* II is built is confirmed by the way in which Eliot's text changed in passing from the manuscript draft to the final version. In the manuscript, for instance, the question "What, are you here?" is closer to *Inferno* XV: "What, are you here, Ser Brunetto?" Again, in the manuscript the poet's persona is rather crudely approximated to Dante's by the phrase "I becoming other." The final text has the subtler "I assumed a double part." The likeness to Brunetto is thus diminished, and a few other details in the manuscript suggestive of *Inferno* XV were similarly pared away later, though verbal reminiscences and gestures were kept. In other words, Eliot started with *Inferno* XV and Brunetto Latini but then moved on to something else. My point is that whilst the way in which the movement changes is typically Eliotian, it was again Dante who suggested both the change and its direction. In fact, this is a splendid instance of Eliot's Dantean and meta-Dantean reading of Dante, of improvement of an invention by means of the invention itself.

We can find some of the clues for this transformation in "What Dante Means to Me," in the manuscript draft of the poem, and in the text such as it was published. First, one will remember that in the essay Eliot alludes to both *Inferno* and *Purgatorio*, omitting any reference to Brunetto. Second, the manuscript draft does not read "some dead master" but "some dead masters." Third, even the final text presents us with "some dead master" who is "both one and many," "a familiar *compound ghost*." This figure is clearly meant to be a stratification of many characters and of their meanings.

If we turn to Dante, we find in his poem a whole series of "dead masters" who stand side by side with Brunetto Latini through the *Inferno* and the *Purgatorio*. All appear to the poet in splendid recognition scenes, all talk about salvation, poetry, politics, and fame. The first and foremost is of course Virgil, the "master" par excellence, "lo mio maestro e 'l mio autore," who guides Dante from the dark wood to the garden of Eden. The "bella scola" of Limbo, which comprises Homer, Horace, Ovid, Lucan, and many other poets of classical antiquity, follows in *Inferno* IV. The indirect presence of Guido Cavalcanti, Dante's friend in the Dolce Stil Nuovo—and the poet from whom Eliot borrowed the opening of *Ash Wednesday*, "Perch'i' no spero di tornar giammai" ("Because I do not hope to turn again")—is felt from *Inferno* X to at least *Purgatorio* XI. Brunetto occupies *Inferno* XV; Sordello, the Mantuan troubadour, *Purgatorio* VI and VII; Bonagiunta da Lucca and Forese Donati appear in *Purgatorio* XXIII–XXIV. The most beautiful recognition scene of the entire Middle Ages takes place in *Purgatorio* XXI–XXII between Dante, Virgil, and Statius. Guinizzelli and Arnaut Daniel speak to Dante, as we have seen, in *Purgatorio* XXVI. Other instances could of course be quoted, but we have enough here to say that Dante's encounters with the "dead masters" sum up the whole cultural tradition of the West such as it might appear to him and that indeed they present us with a problem which is central for Eliot, too, that of the relationship between "tradition" and the "individual talent." For Dante's masters, masters of speech as well as of wisdom and morality and truth, represent the various stages, the various experiences of Western poetry from Homer's and Virgil's epics to Provençal lyric to the Tuscan school in which Dante himself grew up. It is by reinterpreting and fighting against all these—by improving on them—that Dante had to find his own poetic identity as author of the *Comedy*. And they represent various stages of belief, reason, passion, sin, through and against which Dante had to find his own way to salvation as a Christian. The recognition scenes are in fact scenes of self-recognition, in which Dante comes to terms with, and overcomes, his past identities as a writer and a man. I wonder whether this phenomenon may not be hinted at in that interestingly ambiguous passage of *Little Gidding* II where the recognition scene is explicitly, self-consciously announced and described:

> I was still the same
> Knowing myself yet being someone other—
> And he a face still forming; yet the words sufficed
> To compel the recognition they preceded.

Who is the "someone other": Dante the character or the mysterious face which is still forming here? Who is the "myself" whom the poetic persona says he knows? In any case, isn't the recognition preceded by self-knowledge, "knowing myself?" Isn't Eliot describing exactly the real mechanism of the *Divine Comedy* when he says, "I was still the same, / Knowing myself yet being someone other?"

I shall make one final remark about the stratification of master figures in the *Divine Comedy*. In *Inferno* XV, Brunetto is presented as a father figure, "la cara e buona imagine paterna" of the teacher of a long time ago. There are several such father figures in Dante's poem, the first and most important being once more Virgil, followed by Guido Guinizzelli in *Purgatorio* XXVI, where he is called "il padre mio / e delli altri miei miglior che mai / rime d'amor usar dolci e leggiadre" ("the father of me and of the others my betters who ever used sweet and gracious rhymes of love"). Exactly parallel to Brunetto's episode, in canto XV of *Paradiso* Dante meets another important father figure, that of his ancestor Cacciaguida, who consecrates him as a poet-prophet. Finally, the "padre antico," Adam, appears in *Paradiso* XXVI. And I would have readers note that the mysterious interlocutor-ghost of *Little Gidding* declares:

> Since our concern was speech, and speech impelled us
> To purify the dialect of the tribe

Furthermore, it is Guinizzelli who points to Dante the figure of Arnaut Daniel, calling him "il miglior fabbro del parlar materno"—an expression which Eliot used for Ezra Pound in the dedication of *The Waste Land*. It is clear that the interrelated themes of fatherhood, tradition, language, and poetry which run from *Inferno* XV to *Purgatorio* XXVI fascinated Eliot throughout his poetic career.

The last two father figures of the *Divine Comedy* are slightly out of the ordinary. One is St Bernard of Clairvaux, who, after Beatrice's final assumption into the mystical rose next to Mary, prays the Virgin to intercede for Dante so that he may see God. Bernard is a "glorious old man," but he is human. Dante's last father is Our Father Himself: Father, Son, and Holy Ghost, the love that moves the sun and the other stars. It is with this Love, fire and rose that the *Four Quartets* will end.

.   .   .

Let us now go back to *Inferno* XV. Here, we are in the third "girone" of the seventh circle of Hell, the place appointed for the punishment of those who have done Violence against God, against Nature, and against Art. The second group of these are sodomites or homosexuals, who are considered by Dante as violent against Nature, God's daughter. Brunetto belongs to these, all, as he says, being "clerics and great and famous men of letters," a "wretched crowd" "defiled by the same sin." The scenery is undoubtedly infernal, and one that only Dante's imagination could invent. I shall describe it by quoting the summaries which the Temple Classics edition of Dante used by Eliot prefaces to each canto of the *Divine Comedy*. The seventh circle is "a naked plain of burning Sand," limited on one side by the wood of the suicides—"stunted trees, with withered leaves and branches." "A slow eternal Shower of Fire is falling" upon all the groups of the violent:

> Sovra tutto 'l sabbion, d'un cader lento,
> piovean di foco dilatate falde,
> come di neve in alpe senza vento.
> (Over all the great sand, falling slowly,
> rained dilated flakes of fire,
> like those of snow in Alps without a wind.)

After talking to Capaneus—a blasphemer, violent against God—Dante and Virgil "go on, between the burning sand and the wood of Self-murderers, and soon come to a crimson streamlet that gushes forth from the wood and crosses the sandy plain." At the beginning of canto XV, we see that "the crimson stream—whose course is straight across the ring of burning sand, towards the ring of Hell—sends forth a dark exhalation ('il fummo del ruscel') that quenches all the flames over itself and its elevated margins." One will immediately recognize here the source of the fire that dominates in "Little Gidding" II, the fire of the bombs delivered by "the dark dove with the flickering tongue," and the source of the "dead leaves" and the "smoke" of Eliot's second and third terzinas. This is, as we have heard Eliot himself say, "a parallel, by means of contrast," of Dante's scene: Hell-city, fire-bombs, margins-asphalt, "Alps without wind"—"the urban dawn wind." By implication, the violent against Nature of Dante's *Inferno* become the human beings engaged in war.

Walking on one of the margins, "Dante continues to follow his Guide, in silence, till they have got far from the wood, when they meet a troop of spirits coming along the sand by the side of the bank." I would like to draw attention here to the two double similes that Dante employs to describe the background and the first appearance of the "troop of spirits." The first one compares the margins to the dams that the Flemings build between Wissant and Bruges "to repel the sea" and to those the Paduans construct along the Brenta "to defend their villages and castles":

> Quali Fiamminghi tra Guizzante e Bruggia,
> temendo 'l fiotto che 'nver' lor s'avventa,
> fanno le schermo perché 'l mar si fuggia;
> e quali Padoan lungo la Brenta,
> per difender lor ville e lor castelli,
> anzi che Carentana il caldo senta:
> a tale imagine eran fatti quelli,
> tutto che né sí alti né sí grossi,
> qual che si fosse, lo maestro félli.
> (As the Flemings between Wissant and Bruges,
> dreading the flood that rushes towards them,
> make their bulwark to repel the sea;
> and as the Paduans, along the Brenta,
> to defend their villages and castles
> ere Carentana feels the heat;
> in like fashion those banks were formed,
> though not so high nor so large, the master,
> whoever it might be, made them.)

The image is complicated by two details. First, "anzi che Carentana il caldo senta"—before Carinthia feels the heat. This is the heat that melts the snows and causes the river to flood. In other words, Dante is following the course of the Brenta up into Valsugana. But the point is not this. It is, rather, to note how Dante manages to compress allusions to three different regions of Europe in six lines; how in six lines he concentrates cities, flood, sea, river, villages, castles, snow, and heath; how in six lines he draws a comparison between the imaginary margins of an imaginary stream in an imaginary Hell and the earthly reality of the dams built in Flanders and in Veneto. For indeed, as Erich Auerbach said, Dante is the "poet of the secular world," of the earth (Dichter der *irdischen* Welt). Not satisfied with all this, he adds the second detail, specifying that the infernal margins were made by the builder, "whoever he was," neither so high nor so thick as the Flemish or Paduan banks. There is here even an implication that the "maestro" who built them—traditionally the Master Architect, God—might be a lesser, and infernal, artisan. One will understand Eliot's problem when, in talking about his rendering of Dante in *Little Gidding,* he said: "It was chiefly that in this very bare and austere style [Dante's], in which every word has to be 'functional,' the slightest vagueness or imprecision is immediately noticeable."

The second double simile is less complex but equally illuminating:

> quando incontrammo d'anime una schiera
> che venian lungo l'argine, e ciascuna
> ci riguardava come suol da sera
> guardare uno altro sotto nuova luna;
> e sí ver' noi aguzzavan le ciglia
> come 'l vecchio sartor fa ne la cruna.
> (when we met a troop of spirits,
> who were coming alongside the bank;
> and each looked at us, as in the evening
> men are wont to look
> at each other under a new moon;
> and towards us sharpened their vision,
> as an aged tailor does at the eye of his needle.)

Dante, to quote Eliot's own words in the 1929 essay, "is speaking of the crowd in Hell who peered at him and his guide under a dim light." Eliot noticed only the second simile, translating it, "and sharpened their vision (knitted their brows) at us, like an old tailor peering at the eye of his needle." This, he said, had been quite rightly singled out by Matthew Arnold "for high praise." He added: "The purpose of this type of simile is solely to make us *see more definitely* the scene which Dante has put before us in the preceding lines." In fact, the effect of this simile consists in making *us* knit *our* brows to see the scene, that is, to read and relive it more clearly. Eliot neglected the first simile, "and each looked at us as men look at one another under a new moon at dusk." This sketches in the background—the dim light of an evening under a new moon—and introduces human beings, their effort at reaching each other, at seeing, at communicating. It is the first stage of "vision," followed by a narrowing of the focus, the "tailor peering at the eye of his needle." It is the beginning of the recognition scene.

Lines 17–19 of *Inferno* XV are inspired by two passages in Virgil's *Aeneid* which describe the scenery of Aeneas's Dis, his Hell, and the hero's encounter with Dido:

> Ibant obscuri sola sub nocte per umbram
> Perque domos Ditis vacuas et inania regna:
> Quale per incertam lunam sub luce maligna
> Est iter in silvis, ubi caelum condidit umbra
> Iuppiter et rebus nox abstulit atra colorem.
> (Obscure they went through dreary shades, that led
> Along the waste dominions of the dead.
> Thus wander travellers in woods by night,
> By the moon's doubtful and malignant light,
> When Jove in dusky clouds involves the skies,
> And the faint crescent shoots by fits before their eyes.)

> Quam [Dido] Troius heros
> Ut primum iuxta stetit adgnovitque per umbras
> Obscuram, qualem primo qui surgere mense
> Aut videt aut vidisse putat per nubile lunam.
> (Whom when the Trojan hero hardly new,

Obscure in shades, and with a doubtful view
Doubtful as he who sees, through dusky night,
Or thinks he sees, the moon's uncertain light.)

Dante has his own "dead master," from whom he borrows in much the same way as Eliot does from him. An uninterrupted imaginative and thematic chain links these poets: one image from Virgil's recognition scene between Aeneas and Dido in Hell helps Dante introduce his own recognition scene with Brunetto; the Brunetto episode inspires *Little Gidding*. Dante "improves" on Virgil by adding a specific person as the perceiver of the dim scene: the old tailor. Yet the cultural communion between Dante and Virgil is greater than that between Eliot and Dante. Dante can adapt Virgilian similes, use the same figure of speech. Even while drawing his inspiration from Dante, Eliot, as a good modernist, eliminates almost all similes from his rendering of the *Inferno*: in fact, he uses only two in this entire section of *Little Gidding*, both with images of leaves at their centre, "while the dead leaves still rattled on like tin" and "as if blown towards me like the metal leaves." Undoubtedly remembering Dante's and Virgil's comparison between the souls of the dead and fallen leaves (*Inferno* III and *Aeneid* VI), Eliot "improves" on it by introducing a twentieth-century equivalent, the metallic quality that makes his leaves hang between traditional dryness and contemporary bomb debris.

Only one image of the Virgilian-Dantean type is fully kept in *Little Gidding*, once more as if it were the distillation of an entire tradition:

And as I fixed upon the down-turned face
That pointed scrutiny with which we challenge
The first-met stranger in the waning dusk

Eliot skips Dante's old tailor to go, as it were, straight back to the Virgilian root of the icon and modernising it by means of the "stranger." The image, however, is not part of the scenic introduction. It is, rather, worked into the recognition scene itself. The background has changed considerably. The dimness of light, the darkness dominating Dante's scene are now presented directly. Evening has become "the uncertain hour before the morning," and Dante's circle—a spatial entity—is transformed into an image of circular time:

In the uncertain hour before the morning
Near the ending of interminable night
At the recurrent end of the unending

Eliot's ouverture transports us into a different dimension—the approaching end of a specific time, the night, and the intersection of cyclical time and eternity. We shall soon see how this theme might have been suggested or strengthened by Dante.

The scene which opens in *Inferno* XV at line 22 is one of the most memorable episodes of medieval literature. It is prepared by the exceptionally dense background I have tried to outline, but it comes as a sudden and moving surprise like Dante's encounters with Virgil, Farinata, and Ulysses. Dante is suddenly recognized by one of the spirits,

> Who takes him by the skirt; and, on fixing his eyes over the baked and withered figure, he finds it is Brunetto Latini. They speak to each other with great respect and affection, recalling the past, and looking forward to the future under the pressure of separate eternities. Their colloquy has a dark background, which could not be altered; it stands there in deep perennial warmth and beauty.

This is the bare outline of the episode in the version of the Temple Classics, by which, as we shall soon see, Eliot might have been inspired to adopt a central theme. The outline fails to point out the essential movements of the two main figures, Dante and Brunetto, getting closer to each other yet remaining separated both physically and spiritually, as Virgil stands thereby mute almost to the end. Let us try to follow this movement. At first, Dante is eyed by *all* the souls. Almost simultaneously, he is recognized by one of them. This takes him by the hem and cries, "What a marvel!" The whole movement takes no more than three lines, passing from a general view ("famiglia") to one individual ("un"), from vision to recognition ("adocchiato"—"conosciuto") to wonder ("maraviglia") and the familiar gesture of taking the interlocutor by the hem. Brunetto's cry of surprise and his gesture are more eloquent than ten lines of description. This first terzina prepares us for the following. Both the gesture and the exclamation are there to indicate that the figure we are going to meet with Dante is one with whom he has the greatest acquaintance and a very close relationship. Yet Dante the poet keeps us in suspense for one more minute. Surprised by that arm which has reached out for him, Dante fixes his eyes on the man's scorched face. In spite of the "baked features," recognition is full, though not immediate. Like the tailor through the eye of his needle, Dante has to look hard before he actually sees. If intellectual recognition ("intelletto"), the complete, self-aware realization of the identity of his interlocutor, is not instantaneous for Dante, his human reaction—surprise and an attempt at touching the visage of the poor damned ghost—follows without the least pause. Dante's voice brings recognition to us, revealing the speaker's identity: "Siete voi qui, ser Brunetto?" The questioning exclamation is formulated in such a way as to make us realize that Dante is surprised not at meeting Brunetto but at meeting him *here,* in this particular circle of Hell and in this company. If the name and title ("Brunetto" and "ser") are not enough for us to identify the man, he himself will immediately specify "Brunetto Latino," calling Dante "my son" and thus reestablishing the master-pupil, father-son relationship through which we must look at the entire episode and which brings us from Hell back into the past, the world of the living now gone forever.

Brunetto asks Dante to stay with him a little: "let it not displease you if Brunetto Latino turns back a little with you, and lets the train go on." "Ritorna indietro" (turns back) is probably meant both literally and figuratively: Brunetto will stay behind ("dietro") his fellow damned ("la traccia"); at the same time he will turn back to the lost world, to the past. The journey through time is about to begin. Dante offers to sit down with his interlocutor, if Virgil consents, but Brunetto prefers to go on: "Whoever of this flock stops even for an instant must then lie a hundred years without brushing off the fire when it strikes him. Therefore go on: I will come at your skirts, and then will rejoin my band who go lamenting their eternal woes." Here, Brunetto repeats once more, "my son," and shows himself to be keenly aware of time—the present, concentrated in an instant ("punto"); the immediate future as a possibility ("a hundred years"); the eternity of damnation ("etterni danni"). Accepting the situation, Dante indicates the two feelings that dominate him throughout the scene. He dares not, cannot, join Brunetto, but he keeps his head bowed "as one who walks in reverence." We have separation in spite of affection and reverence. The gulf that divides the two men is enormous despite their closeness, past and present. It is one of the most touching, tragic elements of the canto.

Brunetto is an historical figure, and we will understand the pathos of the episode better if we recall a few facts concerning his life and works. A philosopher and a public servant, he was born in Florence ca. 1220 and died there ca. 1294. A Guelph, on returning from an embassy to Alfonso X of Castile in 1260, he learnt that his party had been defeated by the Ghibellines and expelled from Florence. He took refuge in France, where he wrote his major works, *Li livres dou Tresor* and the *Tesoretto,* the former—mentioned in *Inferno* XV—being an encyclopaedia of history, natural science, ethics, rhetoric, and political science, which, soon translated into Italian, became, with Brunetto's other works, a landmark in the cultural history of thirteenth-century Florence. Dante was profoundly influenced by Brunetto's writings both early and late in his career. And it is in this sense that we must understand the figure of Brunetto the "master": as the "maestro" of an entire town in the fields of ethics, politics, and rhetoric. Brunetto returned to Florence after four years of exile. He was married and had several children. This detail is not superfluous, because, as I have said before, Brunetto is condemned to Hell as a sodomite. His homosexuality has been a critical crux for centuries, and I will not go into the history of this debate now. Suffice it to say that recent evidence, together with various allusions in *Inferno* XV, indicates that Brunetto indeed had homosexual tendencies. The law which presides over Dante's other world is inexorable. And one of the sources of pathos in the *Inferno* is precisely the contrast between the sin which condemns certain people and the human sympathy, the admiration, that Dante feels for them. Such is the case with Paolo and Francesca, Farinata, Ulysses, and Brunetto Latini.

Brunetto has a personal, specific identity and is an historical figure. In Eliot's scene, these characteristics have radically changed. The ghost his persona meets is "both intimate and unidentifiable," "familiar" yet "compound," "both one and many": one who has left his body "on a distant shore," a dead master of speech, whom the protagonist "had known, forgotten, half recalled." Although his death on a distant shore might point to Yeats—as would the manuscript draft of the poem, written on the back of Eliot's notes for his lecture on Yeats—it is quite clear that the identity of Eliot's ghost must remain mysterious. Critics have proposed Mallarmé, Dante, Pound, Milton, Swift, Hamlet's father, yet the point surely is that the mystery was willed by the poet himself, precisely because secrecy, as Frank Kermode has taught us, generates poetry and interpretation, establishes hidden connections, makes us see the larger pattern. Eliot's version of the recognition scene confirms this. Dante meets a shadow but presents him as a "cosa salda," made of flesh and blood: face, arm, hand. Eliot meets a man walking, but his appearance is eerie. He is blown, "unresisting," toward the protagonist by "the urban dawn wind" together with the metal leaves. He is "hurried," but also "loitering," suspended between motion and immobility. Even during the recognition scene, he is "a face still forming." He makes no gesture but is only a voice speaking about speech. Space and time have disappeared "at this intersection time / Of meeting nowhere, no before and after." Only the wind and the "pavement" trodden "in a dead patrol" are left. Hence, the recognition is caused—indeed, "compelled"—only by words, and it takes place between two characters whose very appearance is changing under our eyes: the ghost appears as "a face still forming," the protagonist assumes "a double part," crying and hearing "another's voice," "knowing [himself] yet being someone other." There is a curious metamorphic quality to this recognition. The echo of *Inferno* XV is heard only in the background, in the fragments of a sentence or of sound:

> And as I fixed upon the down-turned face
> That pointed scrutiny [...]
> [...] in the brown baked features
> [...] "What! Are *you* here?"
> I said: "The wonder that I feel is easy,
> Yet ease is cause of wonder. [...]"

One sees how words or phrases have been transformed or transposed, at times, as with the "easy" "wonder" ("Qual maraviglia!"), changing the meaning of the episode itself as well as its tone, in a radical "improvement" of the original invention. Following Alan Charity, however, I think that Brunetto's presence is deeper in Eliot's text than a reader at first realizes. Let us therefore ask ourselves what the real meaning of Dante's Brunetto might be. It is a complex one, but if we look with pointed scrutiny we shall see it clearly enough.

In the first place, I would draw attention to the three passages in which Dante describes his dead master directly. In the first of these, Brunetto appears as a "baked aspect" and a "scorched visage." In the second, Dante's memory evokes his "dear and kind, paternal image," "when

in the world, hour by hour," Brunetto taught him "how man makes himself eternal." In the third, at the end of the episode, we see Brunetto, the
once dignified Master of Florence, turn back and seem "like one of those
who run for the green cloth at Verona through the open field; and of
them he who gains, not he who loses." We have three superimposed pic-
tures of Brunetto, two in the present, one in the past. Of the three, the
last—the final shot, as it were—is the most degrading. Those who ran
for the green cloth at Verona (a sort of Palio on foot) ran naked, and
Brunetto disappears on this undignified note. Furthermore, he only
seems like the winner. The present—and it is an eternal present—shows
him consumed, devoured by fire. In the past, his image is reconstituted
as that of the great moral, political, rhetorical teacher of Florence. The
tragic contrast between these images represents the dramatic core of the
episode, as Dante himself realizes when he tells Brunetto: "ché 'n la
mente m'è fitta, ed *or* mi accora" (for in my *memory* is fixed, and *now*
goes to my heart). Memory of the past, reality of the here and now. This
particular sensitivity to time surfaces all over the two key terzinas of
lines 82–87, where "mondo" indicates the past and "ad ora ad ora" the
flowing of opportunities, where "mentr'io vivo" points to Dante's awareness of his being alive versus Brunetto's eternal death and also declares
the poet's intention for the future ("mentre" meaning "until" as well as
"while"). It is here, finally, that Dante alludes to eternity. He remembers
that Brunetto taught him how man makes himself eternal, acquiring,
as the master says in his *Tresor,* that glory which is "second life." This is
in fact one of the two "separate eternities" which the Temple Classics edition of the *Inferno* announces as the central theme of the canto.

    It is Brunetto's eternity. The dead master, whom we have seen keenly
aware of the present instant and of the "etterni danni" of his fellow sinners, and who, in a hurry throughout the episode, repeatedly talks of the
little time at his disposal, constantly looks back ("ritorna 'ndietro") at his
past, projects his own image into the future and foretells Dante's own
future. He recalls his last day, the "vita bella," his untimely death, and in
his last words to Dante recommends to him his work, the *Tresor,* "nel
qual," he says, "io vivo ancora" (in which I still live). Brunetto believes
that the fame one acquires through a work of science and literature
bestows some kind of eternity on a human being. And it is this future
that he envisages for Dante. The long political prophecy of lines 61–78,

in which the Florentine enemies of Dante are abused with unparalleled ferocity and his exile foreshadowed, are prefaced by a memorable sentence:

> Ed elli a me: "Se tu segui tua stella,
> non puoi fallire a glorioso porto"
> (And he to me: "If you follow your star
> You cannot fail of a glorious port").

Star and glorious port are nautical images particularly apt for Dante's journey in the *Comedy*. But they stand for the two things in which Brunetto firmly believes: fortune and fame. Fortune—"fortuna o destino," chance or destiny decreed by God—is mentioned five times by the old master. Fame, honour, glory are reserved by Brunetto to both himself and his pupil, to Florence, and to his fellow sinners: "glorioso porto" and "onor" for Dante; "vecchia fama" for Florence; "literati grandi e di gran fama" for Priscian and Francesco d'Accorso; "nel qual io vivo ancora" for Brunetto's own *Tresor.*

Dante seems to share this ideal of eternity, which, he tells him, he has learnt from Brunetto himself. He even responds to Brunetto's belief in fortune with an attitude which, here as elsewhere in the *Comedy,* looks almost stoical: "This much I would have you know: so conscience chide me not, I am prepared for Fortune as she wills. Such earnest is not strange to my ear; therefore let Fortune whirl her wheel as pleases her, and the yokel his mattock." Yet Dante plays a subtle, and profound, counterpoint against Brunetto's conception of life, death, time, and eternity. When Brunetto asks him what fortune or destiny brings him to Hell before his death, Dante replies with two terzinas, which should teach his master the very lesson of another eternity: in the bright world of the living he went astray in a valley before his age was at the full; only yesterday morning did he turn his back on it; then Virgil appeared, and he is now leading him home "per questo calle," by this path. Home is not Florence; it is the Empyrean of God. Dante's itinerary is totally different from Brunetto's. His past is a "vita serena," the valley of sin, an age not yet full, but he has turned his back to all this "yesterday morning" though he was about to return to it. His present is "this path" that leads him through Hell, Purgatory, and Paradise. His future is "a ca," at home, in

Heaven. This is his destiny and his eternity. Brunetto seems not to understand it at all and launches into the prophecy of the "glorious port." But Dante replies with sadness: if my prayer were all fulfilled, you would not be banished from human nature; that is, you would still be among the living. Brunetto is dead—dead, truly, forever, though he thinks that he still lives in his *Tresor*. It is with infinite "accoramento" that Dante remembers the dear, kind, paternal image of the master who taught him how man makes himself eternal. Past, present, future, eternity all merge here. In the *Four Quartets* Eliot expresses this fusion in the following manner:

> Time present and time past
> Are both perhaps present in time future
> And time future contained in time past.
> If all time is eternally present
> All time is unredeemable.

The clerks and literati "di gran fama" punished here because all guilty of one sin, and the *Tresor* in which Brunetto thinks he still lives, are not without importance. Dante himself will proclaim it aloud—he says—throughout his life. He will write Brunetto's words about the future in his book of memory and keep them to have them glossed, with other texts, by a woman who will know all. This woman is Beatrice, she who makes men blessed. Although what Brunetto says of Dante's future life will not be "glossed" by Beatrice but by Dante's ancestor, Cacciaguida, beginning in the parallel canto XV of the *Paradiso,* the final destination of Dante's journey will be confirmed once more—a "glorious port" indeed, where Dante, travelling the unknown seas of *Paradiso* II, will see "quel mare al qual tutto si move / ciò ch'ella cria e che natura face," that sea toward which moves all that He creates and Nature makes.

   Thus, in spite of the "deep perennial warmth" of their encounter, Dante and Brunetto remain separated by their opposite destinies. And Brunetto runs away like one of those who run for the green cloth at Verona. The canto closes with a realistic and geographic detail which Eliot admired very much. "In making Brunetto so fallen, *run like the winner,* a quality is given to the punishment which belongs only to the greatest poetry," he wrote in his 1929 essay on Dante. In fact, Brunetto

loses—and loses everything—but Eliot is right. The conclusion of
Inferno XV, summing up all the canto's pathos and dramatic contrast, is
a stroke of genius: the genius who invents.

.   .   .

Dante's and Brunetto's two different conceptions of time and eternity
would clearly be important for the T. S. Eliot of the *Four Quartets,* which
are built upon the contrast between a view of time as a simple, continuous, linear development and the view of time held by Christian civilization, as faith into, and perception of, a metahistorical existence. An
intuition of eternity through time is possible only through divine grace,
as the last movement of *The Dry Salvages* makes clear:

> But to apprehend
> The point of intersection of the timeless
> With time, is an occupation for the saint—
> No occupation either, but something given
> And taken, in a lifetime's death in love,
> Ardour and selflessness and self-surrender.

This is the sense of Dante's message to Brunetto, and indeed of his entire
journey, "all'etterno dal tempo," from time to eternity. The message which
the dead master communicates to the poetic persona of *Little Gidding* is
profoundly different from Brunetto's. Brunetto talks of Dante's glorious
future, and Eliot's ghost ironically counterpoints this by offering to "set
a crown upon [a] lifetime's efforts" and reveal "the gifts reserved for *age*."
These gifts are fairly bitter:

> First, the cold friction of expiring sense
> Without enchantment, offering no promise
> But bitter tastelessness of shadow fruit
> As body and soul begin to fall asunder.
> Second, the conscious impotence of rage
> At human folly, and the laceration
> Of laughter at what ceases to amuse.
> And last, the rending pain of re-enactment
> Of all that you have done, and been; the shame

Of motives late revealed, and the awareness
Of things ill done and done to others' harm
Which once you took for exercise of virtue.
Then fools' approval stings, and honour stains.

Instead of a "glorious port," we have here "the shame / Of motives late revealed." The honour reserved to Dante by fortune becomes a stain. The past itself, the work of science, language, and poetry which Brunetto constantly holds before his eyes and projects into eternity, is now forgotten: "These things have served their purpose: let them be."

In this then, which is the only encounter with a human being in the entire *Four Quartets,* Dante's experience is both *followed* and *denied.* Through the recognition scenes of his voyage, Dante learns both what he must avoid and what he must do in order to obtain the vision of God. Brunetto is a typical, tragic, and complex example of what should be avoided. Eliot, who posits the changing of tradition by means of individual talent, seizes on this aspect alone, neglecting the positive instances. Though similar, the two "itineraria in Deum" are grounded upon different perceptions of and reactions to reality, time, and space. Eliot's itinerary in the *Four Quartets* is from consciousness to its denial to the sudden illumination through the negation of wisdom and knowledge and by the way of ignorance:

There is, it seems to us,
At best, only a limited value
In the knowledge derived form experience.

This is the answer given to "the quiet-voiced elders," whose "wisdom" is "only the knowledge of dead secrets":

In order to arrive at what you do not know
You must go by a way which is the way of ignorance.

It is this kind of knowledge, the knowledge of the "via negativa," that the dead, "tongued with fire beyond the language of the living," point to. This is in sum the message brought by the Dantean ghost of *Little Gidding.* Even poetic language which, as the ghost himself says, "impelled us / To purify the dialect of the tribe" as it prompted Brunetto, Guinizzelli,

Cavalcanti, Arnaut Daniel, and Dante to do, is transient. One is re-minded of the passage in *Purgatorio* XI where Oderisi da Gubbio, in showing Dante how the "gloria della lingua" passes from one poet to another, elaborates a first theory of literary transition as "transumption," "agon"—the violent Bloomian conflict which Cimabue's holding of the "field" and Giotto's "cry" of victory announce, and which the "one and the other Guido" fight until a third come, the strongest, Dante, who "will kick them both out of the nest." One thinks of the words of the first father and speaker, Adam, who tells Dante in *Paradiso* XXVI that human language is as mutable as a tree's foliage:

> For last year's words belong to last year's language
> And next year's words await another voice.

Indeed, if "donner un sens plus pur aux mots de la tribu" (to purify the dialect of the tribe) is part of the epitaph which Mallarmé dedicated to Edgar Allan Poe, the sonnet in which this line occurs opens with a quat-rain which, beginning with eternity, narrowing down to a century, and ending with the triumph of death, appears highly significant for the Eliot of the *Four Quartets:*

> Tel qu'en Lui-même enfin l'éternité le change,
> Le Poëte suscite avec un glaive nu
> Son siècle épouvanté de n'avoir pas connu
> Quel la mort triomphait dans cette voix étrange.
> (Such as at last changed into Himself by eternity,
> the Poet rouses with a naked sword
> his century frightened by not having known
> that death triumphed in this strange voice.)

The only solution will be "that refining fire / Where you must move in measure, like a dancer." Purgatorial fire, like that of Guinizzelli and Arnaut Daniel, this has no longer anything to do with the rain of fire which scorches Brunetto's visage. Dawn is coming, and the familiar com-pound ghost, like the ghost of Hamlet's father in that uncertain, enig-matic recognition scene I have examined in the first chapter of this volume, disappears—perhaps "for the day confin'd to fast in fires":

The day was breaking. In the disfigured street
He left me, with a kind of valediction,
And faded on the blowing of the horn.

And Dante, whose invention inspires Eliot, finds himself "improved"
by Dante, Mallarmé, and Shakespeare.

CHAPTER FIVE

Oedipus and Lear

Recognition and Nothingness

Sophocles' *Oedipus Rex* is, for Aristotle, the superlative example of recognition. His reason is that it occurs in parallel with the *peripeteia* (the plot reversal) and grows "from the events themselves." Few of us would have any problems with this. The play's (astonishingly lean) fifteen hundred lines scroll quickly before our eyes, unfolding into a recognition which the spectator has been expecting from the beginning of the tragedy. The following are the basic stages in this extraordinarily dense plot and rapid unravelling, almost more akin to a clock mechanism than a work of theatre.

In the "Prologue," as it could be defined, we find Oedipus and the Priest discussing the situation in Thebes. Why, Oedipus asks the Priest as representative of the city, is the air crammed with the incense, laments, and supplication of those whom he, as king, calls his children? The Priest informs him of the epidemic raging throughout and begs him to save his city once again, as he has saved it in the past from the threats of the Sphinx. Oedipus has already sent his brother-in-law Creon to seek advice of the Delphic oracle, and he arrives at that moment with her reply: there is something impure (a *miasma*) in Thebes, Phoebus states, which must be purged away. When he is pressed for details, Creon adds that a man must be exiled or killed "since that blood scourges the city." The blood he alludes to is that of Laius, the previous king of Thebes, who was killed by bandits while on a pilgrimage, some years before Oedipus was

111

crowned. Only one man survived the ambush, and no further investi-
gations were made, as Thebes was then busy trying to avert the atten-
tions of the Sphinx. At this Oedipus declares he will clarify (show, reveal:
phanō) the whole episode. In the *parados* the Chorus invokes the word
of Zeus, newly arrived from Delphi, then prays to Athena, Artemis, and
Phoebus, bewails the pestilence afflicting the city, and again invokes
Apollo and Bacchus.

In the first episode, Oedipus orders an enquiry into the death of
Laius, his wife Jocasta's first husband. The blind Tiresias, summoned by
Oedipus, now arrives, led by a slave. Initially he refuses to answer Oedi-
pus, but when the king rounds on him, accusing him of having ordered
Laius's death, he informs him that he himself, Oedipus, is tainting Thebes:
"I say you are the murderer of the king / whose murderer you seek."
Moreover, he adds, Oedipus lives, unwittingly, "in foulest shame . . . with
those [he] loves." Understandably beside himself, Oedipus accuses him
of being in league with his brother-in-law Creon, adding, for good measure, that his powers of prophecy seem less than infallible: after all it was
he, Oedipus, and not Tiresias, who "by wit alone" solved the riddle of
the Sphinx. Tiresias then predicts the calamities to come, exiting with a
last allusion to the crime:

> I tell you, king, this man, this murderer
> (whom you have long declared you are in search of,
> indicting him in threatening proclamation
> as murderer of Laius)—he is here.
> In name he is a stranger among citizens
> but soon he will be shown to be a citizen
> true native Theban, and he'll have no joy
> of the discovery: blindness for sight
> and beggary for riches his exchange,
> he shall go journeying to a foreign country
> tapping his way before him with a stick.
> He shall be proved father and brother both
> to his own children in his house; to her
> that gave him birth, a son and husband both;
> a fellow sower in his father's bed
> with that same father that he murdered.

In the first stasimon the Chorus speculates as to the murderer's identity, invokes the "voice" from Parnassus, comments on the quarrel between Oedipus and Tiresias, and compares the wisdom of Zeus and Apollo with man's "lack of distinct judgment."

The second episode is the quarrel between Oedipus and Creon, Jocasta's brother. Creon has manipulated Tiresias, Oedipus insists, in order to leave the field free for Creon to take over. Power politics are the inevitable terms of reference for a *tyrannos;* hybris clouds his mind. Creon roundly denies the accusation, pointing out the far from negligible fact that, as the third in command, he already wields considerable power: "As it stands now / the prizes are all mine—and without fear": the mere name of king would add, de facto, nothing. The Chorus attempts to dissuade Oedipus from killing Creon and, at the entrance of Jocasta, invokes her "help / to lay the quarrel."

In the third episode Oedipus tells Jocasta that Creon and Tiresias accuse him of Laius's murder. Jocastra tries to calm him, and, at the beginning of the dialogue between them—a crucial point in the plot—gives details of his killing. To prove the fallibility of prophecy, she explains that Laius had been told by an oracle that his death would be at the hands of a son of theirs, whereas in actual fact he was killed by "foreign highway robbers" at a three-way crossroads. Moreover, that very newborn son who should have killed his father was bound by the ankles and abandoned on a "pathless hillside." At these details Oedipus asks tremblingly for a physical description of Laius and of his train and begins to realize "with deadly fear / that the old seer had eyes." At Jocasta's insistence he explains that a "curious chance" had once occurred, whereby he was one day accused by a drunkard of being a bastard and not the son of Polybus and Merope of Corinth. His parents reassured him, but "this thing rankled always," and he finally went to Delphi to consult Apollo: his answer was that Oedipus was to face "desperate horrors": to lie with his mother and kill his father. He fled from Corinth immediately, on his way passing through the very place Jocasta had just mentioned, at the Phocis crossroads where Laius, she informs him, had been killed. A carriage had then arrived, bearing a man of exactly Jocasta's description; on the man's trying to force him off the road, Oedipus fought and killed him, with all his retinue. Hence, he was indeed guilty of Laius's death and did indeed "pollute the bed of him [he] killed": he is thus left with no alternative to exile, the penalty he himself had imposed on Laius's murderer. Nor would he ever dare set foot in Corinth, to avoid the "deadly taint" of the rest of the prophecy.

Jocasta informs him of one surviving witness, the one slave to escape the slaughter, who, on Oedipus's coronation, begged to be sent into the fields as shepherd, "so he might see the city / as far off as he might." There is, Oedipus realizes, one vital detail he can confirm: if Laius was killed by *robbers,* in the plural, then he, who was alone, is innocent. His wife points out that he cannot but confirm what so many had heard and that in any case no faith can be put in prophecies: Apollo had predicted that Laius would be killed by his own son, who had in fact died before him. In the second stasimon the Chorus speaks of hybris and tyranny, invokes *dikē,* and deplores humanity's lack of faith in oracles.

In the fourth episode, as Jocasta is preparing a sacrifice to Apollo, a messenger arrives from Argos, announcing that Polybus has died and that the city names Oedipus as king. Jocasta and Oedipus rejoice at this confirmation that his father "is dead in the course of nature," not at his son's hand; Oedipus, however, is still reluctant to go to Argos, fearing "his mother's bed," the second part of the prophecy. At this point the messenger reveals that he is not the son of Polybus and Merope but was given to him by another shepherd, of the house of Laius, who had found him as a newborn baby, the tendons of his feet pierced and fettered— hence his name—on the slopes of Mount Cithaeron. The shepherd, the Chorus points out, must therefore be the same man who was present at Laius's killing, whom Oedipus had already sent for. Jocasta, in a flash of understanding, begs Oedipus to go no further in his enquiry, but he refuses "to let be / the chance of finding out the whole thing clearly." With a desperate "God keep you from the knowledge of who you are!" Jocasta flees in wild grief, while Oedipus simply repeats that his origins must be discovered, at the cost of plunging his wife into the social shame of having married below herself: "for she has all a woman's high-flown pride," while he is content to be "a child of Fortune," of Tykhe. The Chorus, in the third stasimon, muses that he may be the child of Pan, of Bacchus, or Apollo himself.

The fifth episode, however, brings the old Theban shepherd and the information that Oedipus is indeed the child he was given on Mount Cithaeron; the child was royal born, the son of Laius and Jocasta, who

wanted to be rid of him on account of the prophecy that he would slay
his own father. Oedipus is now in full possession of the truth. Everything
must come to pass: "Light of the sun, let me / look upon you no more
after today! / I who first saw the light bred of a match / accursed, and
accursed in my living / with them I lived with, cursed in my killing." He
leaves. In the fourth stasimon the Chorus comments on human destiny:

> Oh generations of men, how I
> count you as equal with those who live
> not at all!
> What man, what man on earth wins more
> of happiness than a seeming
> and after that turning away?
> Oedipus, you are my pattern of this,
> Oedipus, you and your fate!
> Luckless Oedipus, whom of all men
> I envy not at all.

In the sixth episode we learn that Jocasta has hanged herself and Oedipus blinded himself with his wife's clasp. When he returns onstage for
the last time, and is reproved by the Chorus for taking his own sight, his
terrifying reply is as follows:

> What I have done here was best done—don't tell me
> otherwise, do not give me further counsel.
> I do not know with what eyes I could look
> upon my father when I die and go
> under the earth, nor yet my wretched mother—
> those two to whom I have done things deserving
> worse punishment than hanging. Would the sight
> of children, bred as mine are, gladden me?
> No, not these eyes, never. And my city,
> its towers and sacred places of the Gods,
> of these I robbed my miserable self
> when I commanded all to drive *him* out,
> the criminal since proved by God impure
> and of the race of Laius.

To this guilt I bore witness against my people?
No. If there were a means to choke the fountain
of hearing I would not have stayed my hand
from locking up my miserable carcase,
seeing and hearing nothing; it is sweet
to keep our thoughts out of the range of hurt.

Cithaeron, why did you receive me? why
having received me did you not kill me straight?
And so I had not shown to men my birth.

Polybus and Corinth and the house,
the old house that I used to call my father's—
what fairness you were nurse to, and what foulness
festered beneath! Now I am found to be
a sinner and a son of sinners. Crossroads,
and hidden glade, oak and the narrow way
at the crossroads, that drank my father's blood
offered you by my hands, do you remember
still what I did as you looked on, and what
I did when I came here? O marriage, marriage!
you bred me and again when you had bred
bed children of your child and showed to men
brides, wives and mothers and the foulest deeds
that can be in this world of ours.

Come—it's unfit to say what is unfit
to do.—I beg of you in God's name hide me
somewhere outside your country, yes, or kill me,
or throw me into the sea, to be forever
out of your sight. Approach and deign to touch me
for all my wretchedness, and do not fear.
No man but I can bear my evil doom.

Creon arrives, and Oedipus asks him to banish him and "to her that lies
inside that house give burial." He also begs him to take care of his daughters, and that he might be allowed to touch them once more. Antigone
and Ismene enter, and Oedipus asks to be left alone with them; he then
refuses to be parted from them until Creon curtly orders him, "Do not

seek to be master in everything, / for the things you mastered did not follow you throughout your life." With this, the tragedy of Oedipus *Tyrannos,* of Oedipus the crushed and ruined king, comes to an end.

Two aspects immediately emerge from this plot. First, the recognition in the fifth episode is not recognition in the normal, Aristotelian sense of the term. It is not a person Oedipus "recognises" but a fact: that he himself, the investigator, is the assassin. He discovers himself, his origins, his birth, his *seed,* as he himself defines it. Second, the whole tragedy is rushing toward this recognition: in other words, with a virtuosity which probably has no parallel in literature, the poet has managed to sublimate the entire narrative structure to one ongoing mechanism of recognition.

The *gnōsis,* the knowledge which according to Aristotle is produced by the act of recognition, is developed and *discussed* from the beginning of the tragedy. For Oedipus, the whole plot is "a movement from ignorance to knowledge" (as Aristotle's definition of anagnorisis goes); he proceeds by blinding illuminations or step by gradual step: from pits of deep crisis to creeping awareness (the crossroads, the news from the Argos messenger, the old shepherd's revelation). A paradigm of the connection between *hamartia,* the unwitting, tragic error, and recognition, Oedipus incarnates the action of *anagnōrizein* itself, the process whereby knowledge slowly emerges; and his fate consists in reenacting, through increasing degrees of awareness, the same steps which had taken him, unknowingly, down into the black pit of his being—toward the point of contact with his mother and his father. In this sense his fate is a recognition, the anagnorisis of something already within him.

The fundamental point here is this process of *gnōrisis*: not *gnōsis, savoir,* but the actual making, the building up, of knowledge: *connaître.* Ruthlessly systematic, this is created by three distinct but ultimately interconnected means, respectively verbal, structural, and thematic, which I shall deal with in that order.

The words of *Oedipus Rex* are, of course, extremely important. They reveal character, as in all plays, but here the pressing counterpoint of dialogue enacts the action itself. It is through words, questions, that Oedipus discovers the truth. But words are of different types, divine and human, with a different value. The word of the gods—*phatis* and *phama*—is the "voice" of Delphi. The pestilence in Thebes, it announces, is caused by a *miasma,* a contamination that requires purification: the

discovery of Laius's murderer and his exile from the city. But the Lord
who dwells in Delphi, as Heraclitus had said, "neither states nor hides:
he *semainei,* he signifies." The Theban Chorus protests, insisting it should
be Phoebus, who sent the oracle, to *say* who the murderer is. But the
gods have their own times and seasons, and no man, as Oedipus replies,
can "put compulsion on the gods / against their will." The god's voice is
mysterious, needs interpreting, and Tiresias who, as Oedipus himself
recognises, is "versed in everything, / things teachable, and things not
to be spoken, / things of the heaven and earth-creeping things," offers
the interpretation. What he knows, however, is that Oedipus himself is
the murderer and, in words as allusive as those of the oracle, foretells his
future, setting present vision against coming darkness (a darkness Oedipus himself speaks of in the same passage): he condemns the false
"haven" of Oedipus's marriage and his "grim equality" with his children.
Tiresias's words, as he himself maintains, are inspired by Loxias, Apollo
the "Oblique."

Against this divine, ambiguous word is set that of humanity, although one of the play's startling paradoxes is that it is through the latter,
the words of the messenger from Argos and the old shepherd, that the
divine word is explained and endorsed, with the further irony that they
are set in motion by Oedipus himself, who, with the drive of a private
investigator, indefatigably interrogates and comments. It is his word, that
of the *tyrannos,* the supreme authority, that orders the enquiry and claims
its right to speak. Yet his word is dubious, ambiguous, amphibological,
as critics have underlined. He says one thing and implies another, con-
cealing a truth which is unknown to him but not to us. When Creon
speaks, for example, of the robbers (plural) who killed Laius, Oedipus
responds by asking how "*a* robber [would] dare a deed like this, were he
not helped," thereby unwittingly condemning himself. Then when Oedipus announces he will fight "in [Laius's] defense / as for my father," tragic
irony has no further to go.

In Oedipus's words human and divine language, initially totally
distinct, gradually merge, while, as Vernant writes, "on the steps of the
theatre, the spectators occupy almost the privileged position of the
gods, simultaneously understanding the two opposite discourses." At
the beginning of the play Oedipus states to the Chorus, *egō phanō,* "I shall
bring the criminal to light," but also "I shall reveal myself a criminal."
The tragedy shows how this ambiguity of his, the enigma he represents,

is resolved by reversal. This is of two kinds, as Knox has pointed out: in the first, the meaning of the terms describing Oedipus are systematically reversed. From the hunter pursuing his prey over the mountainside, he becomes the wild beast, bellowing his blind way across Mount Cithaeron. In the second type, the terms describing him at the peak of his glory are gradually shifted to the gods: at the beginning it is Oedipus who is called "sovereign" by the Priest; later the Chorus applies it to Zeus. In the first line of the play, Oedipus addresses the suppliant Thebans like a father to his children; two hundred lines later, the Chorus refers to Zeus in the same way.

Then there is, famously, the name Oedipus itself: *Oidipous*, he with a swollen foot (*oidos*), but also he who knows (*oida*) the enigma of the foot. Who, the Sphinx asks, is the being who is simultaneously *dipous, tripous, tetrapous,* two-, three-, and four-footed? This poses no mystery for *Oidipous:* it is man, he himself. His final question will therefore be: then who am I? The Sphinx's enigma constitutes the answer: he is the man who identifies both with his own children and with his own father—child, adult, and old man at the same time. He is the answer, yet the answer is an enigma.

If we then move from this densely patterned verbal plot to the play's macro-plot, this, too, reveals the same reversal mechanism, again through words. This is the structural means referred to above, articulated into three levels. The first is the level of action taking place in front of our eyes—the enquiry, the prophecy, the quarrel with Creon and Tiresias, the dialogue with Jocasta, the arrival of the messenger from Argos, and the arrival of the old shepherd. The action rediscovers Oedipus's past, of which he knows nothing (his birth and abandonment on account of the prophecy), at the same time also revealing the facts immediately predating the action, of his known and recent past. The episode with the Sphinx is recalled by the Priest at the beginning of the play and used by Oedipus to taunt Tiresias; Oedipus's relatively recent arrival in Thebes is mentioned by himself, in the first episode; the Sphinx is again evoked by the Chorus, and toward the middle of the play Oedipus speaks of his putative parents, Polybus and Merope. Jocasta adds further details: the crossroads, the murder of Laius, the prophecy regarding Laius's son, and the only witness, the old servant.

From the moment the Argos messenger arrives, these three levels—action, past, and immediate past—begin to merge, finally exploding in recognition with the arrival of the old shepherd. The plot has two singular details, both of them crucial moments of *méconnaissance,* of nonrecognition. The first is the superimposition of two parallel oracles: Jocasta informs Oedipus of the oracle announcing that Laius would be killed by his own son. Immediately afterward Oedipus tells Jocasta of an oracle from Apollo announcing that he would kill his own father and lie with his mother, and Jocasta responds by citing the first one as proof of the fallibility of oracles generally. The two correspond precisely, of course, to Tiresias's allusion to his relationship of "foulest shame" with "those [he] love[s] best" and to his final, terrifying prophecy, yet Oedipus, master solver of enigmas, fails to relate the two oracles in any way and completely overlooks the clues. He is unable, at this point, to recognize the truth.

It is difficult to believe that this is simply because Sophocles wants to add more fuel of dramatic tension to the final blaze of recognition. In my opinion, this nonrecognition serves both to underline Oedipus's inability to perform some simple mathematics and reach the answer four, and also, at a more significant level, (as André Green has pointed out), to demonstrate that he is "in denial," blacking out this particular truth until events force it on his consciousness. Oedipus is the man who can put *dipous, tripous,* and *tetrapous* together and, in an instant's illumination, recognize the infinite they conceal, the human being. Now, however, he takes one cautious step at a time, proceeding with carping diligence, demanding eyewitnesses and firsthand proof. Mere oracles, in total agreement to boot, are not sufficient. He cannot afford to accept their agreed truth because it would endorse what Tiresias had obliquely told him: he is indeed his father's murderer and his mother's husband. This can, of course, be read as Freud's archetypal Oedipal complex (or rather, as Guido Paduano has perceptively pointed out, its inverse: when both Oedipus and Jocasta refute the oracle, Jocasta pronounces the famous words which form the bedrock of Freudian critics: "As to your mother's marriage-bed, don't fear it. / Before this, in dreams too, as well as oracles, / many a man has lain with his own mother"). Equally, we could, with Lévi-Strauss, see it within the context of the whole Theban myth, of a culture, that is, which considers humanity autochthonous and thus has to find an explanation for the fact that present-day human beings are the result of a male-female union. In either case, what Oedipus undoubtedly represents is the icon of the man who rejects the truth at the very moment he is trying to bring it out. He is quick to pick up Jocasta's allusion to the crossroads, realising that what she describes is what he has performed, and is anxious to know the number of killers. Like Jocasta, however, he ignores the oracles, and neither of them thinks to wonder why the old servant, the sole survivor of the ambush, on his return to Thebes begs Jocasta, as she herself tells Oedipus, to be sent as far away from the city as possible.

Oedipus makes sufficient connection to fear he may be Laius's murderer but not his son, overlooking, in this supreme *méconnaissance,* the crucial "forensic" evidence: his perforated foot. In this same exchange between them, Jocasta explains that Laius's wretched son had been abandoned with his ankles tied, a detail Oedipus stolidly ignores both now and thereafter, when the Argos messenger gives his description of the child found on Mount Cithaeron: "Why do you speak of that old pain?" is his only reaction. The messenger replies that he himself had "loosed" his "pierced and fettered" ankles: hence Oedipus's name. The two descriptions of the feet are not identical, but Oedipus should be aware—in his own flesh—of the real meaning of Jocasta's euphemism. In other words, for Oedipus the nonrecognition is in two phases, the second confirming and compounding the first. From line 718 to 1034, a full fifth of the tragedy, Oedipus forgets himself, his own name, his own feet. He reproaches the old man for reminding him of "that old pain," yet the "old pain" he has chosen to forget is precisely the clue which would solve the enigma.

All this is taking place in a tragedy in which Oedipus represents the new and rational human "science," grounded in experience, research, and enquiry. To summarise the cogent argument of Mario Vegetti, Oedipus is he who, through reason (*gnōmē*), pursues his *historia*, exploits the *kairos*, the right moment, analyses the signs (*semēia*), and concludes in *heuresis*, discovery. He is the paradigm of knowledge—the learning (*mathēsis*) and discovery which lead to certain knowledge (*saphēs*). As such, he is the opposite of the seemingly ultra-rational Jocasta, who denies the validity of prophecy, declaring roundly that oracles should be brought to (judicial) account, though her rejection of all prediction (*pronoia*) because inevitably lacking certainty (*saphēs*), smacks of the decidedly inconsistent. Jocasta considers the human sphere dominated by chance and destiny and is set against any form of knowledge: "God keep you from the knowledge of what you are!"

At the same time, this *saphēs* of her husband's is in contrast with Tiiresias's *alētheia,* that is, truth begotten as a natural human gift, and not created through enquiry and research. Tiresias, as he himself states, nurtures the truth; moreover, as the Chorus endorses, he is the only man in whom it is innate. His *aletheia* is a total and instant vision of things and of the past which produces them. A "master of truth" of the archaic age, Tiresias is a majestic if primitive fossil of the sovereignty which sets itself over and against Oedipus's new "tyranny."

It is this truth which undermines all Oedipus's certainty, although only through him is it evoked and fulfilled. Tiresias is better acquainted with the past than the future, and Oedipus has every right to underline his inability to "glean" the Sphinx's meaning. Tiresias represents humanity's interpretation of Apollo's wisdom, but this is void of fact and has to be completed by Oedipus's enquiry. In berating Tiresias he accuses him of being "blind in mind and ears / as well as in eyes," and, ultimately, in his "skill," his prophetic art. Tiresias lacks sensitivity, *aisthēsis,* and therefore, according to Oedipus the empiricist, *nous,* wit. Nor is he a god, for, as Xenophanes informs us, a god would "see in complete wise, hear in complete wise, and think in complete wise" (it should be noted, incidentally, that this is a change of heart in Oedipus, who had previously apostrophised Tiresias as being "versed in everything, / things teachable and things not to be spoken, / things of the heaven and earth-creeping things").

The point is precisely this: what exactly is *sophia,* wisdom, and what store should be set by rationality? The Chorus formulates the question, commenting, in the first stasimon, when Tiresias and Oedipus have crossed swords:

> Truly Zeus and Apollo are wise
> and in human things all knowing;
> but amongst men there is no
> distinct judgment, between the prophet
> and me—which of us is right.
> One man may pass another in wisdom.

Tiresias's knowledge is archaic: that of Oedipus, the knowledge current in the Athens of Pericles, the philosophy of Anaxagoras, the new historiography of Thucidides, the critical spirit of the Sophists, the new science of medicine—that same discipline which, in Sophocles' own period, had failed to cure the plague in Athens, so that the statue of Aesculapius had been brought to the city (and stood, apparently, in Sophocles' own house). Thus, Oedipus's *saphēs* culminates in the discovery of the scapegoat, the *pharmakos*, which is to purify Thebes and rout the pestilence: he is both the *miasma* and the medicine, the subject and object of knowledge.

The conflict emerges, then, of different types of knowledge: an enquiry into truth, wisdom, and science constituting the theme through which Sophocles constructs his recognition, the move from ignorance to knowledge. The oracle of Apollo comes from Delphi: the Delphic motto is *gnōthi seauton*, know yourself. In *Oedipus Rex* we find both meanings: "man, recognise that you are a mere man," as the Chorus concludes in the fourth stasimon; and "man, know yourself." And this is precisely what Oedipus wants to know: who he is, what his *seed* is, what his origins are. Oedipus pursues the aim set out by the Delphic motto at first unconsciously, then deliberately, as if his "self" were external to man, an object of enquiry to be arrived at through deduction, proof, and signs— in short, a natural phenomenon to be examined and explained by science. But on discovering himself both investigator and investigated, *zētōn* and *zētoumenon*, Oedipus is moving proleptically toward the meditation and self-reflection which characterises philosophy as Aristotle defines it in the *Metaphysics: zētoumenē epistēmē*, researched science. The tragedy of Oedipus's ironic *gnōthi seauton*—the tragedy of *Oedipus Rex*—lies in showing how difficult it is to reach this knowledge rationally, how in fact impossible if man does not journey into himself and, as it were, bend over onto himself as biblical characters do (since man is not simply a natural phenomenon). And furthermore, when that knowledge is attained, the prize is nothingness: obscurity, duality, and the mesh of contradictions and unspeakable horror that strangles the roots of self (father and mother), blinding him while conferring a ghastly "immortality." "No sickness and no other thing will kill me," the sightless, shattered Oedipus baldly states: he has eaten of the tree of knowledge, and "is as God."

In *Oedipus at Colonus* the ninety-year-old Sophocles makes Oedipus's tragic awareness and destiny constitute the safety of Athens, but this is as yet a far-off point of arrival. *Oedipus Rex*, the tragedy of power and knowledge, "simply" presents the thudding weight of this knowledge and its effects. "Alas, how terrible is wisdom when / it brings no profit to the man that's wise! / This I knew well, but had forgotten it, / else I would not have come here," Tiresias himself observes at the beginning of the play. Tiresias is speaking here of his own situation while alluding to that of Oedipus at the end of the play; for him, knowledge is a burden—to the extent that even he, the all-seeing seer, has, in his extraordinary sentence, *forgotten his own awareness of it*. This is perhaps the first time we hear it pronounced in Western literature, and apprehend one of humanity's main psychological mechanisms: the oblivion in which we bury, out of sight of our conscience, the unbearable heaviness of knowledge.

Jocasta's turn soon comes. When she suddenly grasps who Oedipus is, she exclaims: "God help you! God keep you from the knowledge of who you are!" the precise opposite of the Delphic injunction to "know yourself." It is reiterated by the Chorus, toward the end of the tragedy, when the blind Oedipus reappears on the scene: "Unhappy in your mind and your misfortune: / would I had never known you!" Here, however, the exclamation is ambiguous and could equally mean: "Unhappy in your mind and your misfortune: / would you had never known!" In the first reading, the Chorus is rejecting its own share in knowledge; in the second, echoing Jocasta's words, it regrets Oedipus's share: that knowledge had ever been necessary. In the second, moreover, Oedipus's intellect equals his destiny, an expression which, in the context of a general rejection of knowledge, would be significant indeed.

The Chorus's withdrawal from its share of the burden has actually already occurred, in the awesome fourth stasimon in which the generations of mortals are defined as equal to "nothing." "O child of Laius, / would I had never seen you!" the Chorus had cried, and the field had suddenly widened. The Chorus is speaking for the whole of Thebes, the polis, and thus for the people of Athens, and extends to them the idea of knowledge, here represented by its "object," Oedipus, as a burden. Will the public, too, on acquiring its own knowledge, discover the abyss of its own self? When Oedipus, his eyes freshly pierced, the bleeding eyeballs gushing and staining his beard, reappears for the last time, the Chorus pronounces a lament in which horror has paralysed all will to know or enquire:

This is a terrible sight for men to see!
never found a worse!

Poor wretch, what madness [*mania*] came upon you!
What evil spirit [*daimon*] leaped upon your life
to your ill-luck—a leap beyond man's strength!
Indeed I pity you, but I cannot
look at you, though there's so much I want to ask
and much to learn and much to see.
I shudder at the sight of you.

Is this, then, our fate for being party to Oedipus's secret, for acquiring knowledge, for passing from ignorance to knowledge? Does recognition mean that we, too, like Tiresias, now wish to forget the knowledge of knowledge, accepting the oblivion of ignorance? Or do we edge into madness, elbowed by the *daimon*? All this is certainly one of the truths *Oedipus Rex* recites. The truth in the character of Oedipus, however, is a different matter. In this scene with the Chorus, Oedipus laments both the tortures of the flesh and the *memory* of his ills, "stabbing pain and memory," the awareness of a knowledge which is now undeniable and indelible—the memory confirming that, even at the end of the tragedy, there is no rejection of knowledge, on Oedipus's part: he in fact continues to champion knowledge as he has done throughout the whole grim unfolding. His curses are, rather, for the man who "stole [him] from death" as a child; he has blinded himself and desires deafness, too, because "it is sweet / to keep our thought out of the range of hurt"—and certainly "sweet" to put aside all knowledge—but he accepts his destiny, knowing he is a stain on the entire community. Interestingly, it is now, when he is blind and powerless, that he thinks of his daughters, thanks Creon for taking pity on him, and appreciates the Chorus's kindness and compassion. Equally interesting, this wider recognition is emblematically expressed in the way in which he "recognises" them, despite his blindness: "Your care is not unnoticed. I can know [*gignōskō saphōs*] / your voice, although this darkness is my world." He is recognising the human "voice" through which the Chorus has represented the city of Thebes from the first lines of the play, when it was a tyrant-to-subject relationship: if not as a god, certainly as the "first" among men. Now Oedipus is a man among men, and a "model," as the Chorus states in the fourth stasimon, a *paradeigma*, of human fate and misery.

It is now very clear both why Aristotle chose this recognition in *Oedipus Rex* as his paradigm and why Freud saw in this particular character from myth the incarnation of what he considered one of the most fundamental mechanisms of our subconscious. Oedipus's passing from ignorance to knowledge is a debate on knowledge itself, on truth, enquiry, reason, and the value of self-awareness. The *méconnaissance* and recognition of Oedipus, the rational seeker of truth, represent the triumph and defeat of knowledge and self-knowledge both as the process of knowing, *connaître,* and as knowledge in itself, *savoir,* since knowledge in itself has no intrinsic value. Odysseus re-*cognises* himself, his dead mother, his son, his wife, and his father. Oedipus re-*cognises* himself, his father, his mother, his wife, and his children. Odysseus's long absence makes his recognition a sublimation of the feelings and prime human needs; Oedipus's unknowing presence turns his recognition into a curse on the whole of human kind. Odysseus's recognition fills a void for us, fills us with enthusiasm for knowledge, and makes us one and many; the recognition of Oedipus drains off our wholeness, anathematises knowledge, and makes us "equal to nothing." Catharsis becomes an unbearable burden, and an unbearable question: are we, too, like Oedipus?

·   ·   ·

The best answer is possibly through my original question: can Sophocles' invention be improved on? The Oedipus myth in Western literature has been so subtly pursued, over such a distance, by Guido Paduano in his *Lunga storia di Edipo Re,* that the need for subsequent travellers is largely superseded. Let me take a more oblique route, with a brusquer leap from Sophocles to Shakespeare than in my first chapter. This time, though *Oedipus Rex* is traditionally (in Freud's subconscious, too) associated with *Hamlet,* I shall take *King Lear.* This is in part because the last scene of *Oedipus Rex* that I examined, the blind Oedipus's recognition of the voice of the Chorus, steals a two-thousand-year march on the scene in which the blind Gloucester recognises the voice of King Lear ("I know that voice. . . . The trick of that voice I do well remember"), but also because I consider *King Lear* the inverted response made by the Renaissance—and therefore modernity—to the political and gnoseological questions put by *Oedipus Rex.*

Let me begin with the basic plot mechanisms of recognition. *Lear* is the tragedy of an old *tyrannos* who, unlike Oedipus, signs away his kingdom in order to "unburthen'd, crawl toward death." Beguiled by his own narcissism, the blandishments of his two "bad" daughters Goneril and Regan, and the obdurate silence of the "good" daughter Cordelia, he divides up his kingdom among Goneril, Regan, and their respective husbands, banishing the third, his youngest, and the faithful Kent who attempts to reason with him. He is quickly disabused: Goneril and Regan lose no time in stripping him of followers and assets generally, finally turning him out-of-doors. Crazed with grief, he wanders over the country like a beggar, with only his Fool and the disguised Kent. His reason finally cracks in the storm scene on the heath; the repudiated Cordelia, with her husband the king of France, then returns in a failed attempt to save him. In the specular subplot, the old Duke of Gloucester is hoodwinked by his illegitimate son Edmund into believing his legitimate son Edgar is plotting against him; Edgar is turned out and forced to wander the country, half-naked, as Poor Tom the beggar. In return for helping their father, Gloucester is blinded by Lear's daughters. The two old men meet near Dover as Cordelia is disembarking, to come to her father's assistance with French troops; Edmund, in the meantime, passes the time playing off the two sisters in highly charged erotic interrelations. Cordelia finds her father, is defeated by Edmund's army, is taken prisoner with Lear, and is finally killed. Edgar challenges Edmund to a duel after the death of their father and kills him; the play ends with Lear's own death.

The last two acts of *Lear* contain four scenes of recognition: one between Lear and Gloucester, which I mentioned above (IV, iv); one between Lear and Cordelia (IV, vii); one between Edgar and Edmund, during their duel (V, iii), (and, recognition within recognition, Edgar's account of his self-disclosure to Gloucester before the latter's death); and, last, one shortly before the very end of the play, between Kent and Lear (V, iii). I shall look at some of the relevant elements here. Lear's tragedy immediately presents itself as based on *hamartia,* in Lear's wishing to retain "The name and all th'addition to a king" even as he gives up real power, and when, blinded by anger, he ignores Cordelia's sincerity and Kent's attempt to help him "see better"; when, as Kent puts it, he "kills[s] the physician, and [the] fee bestow[s] / Upon the foul disease," and rejects all his "paternal care, / Propinquity and property of blood"—his own *philia*—with regard to Cordelia. Through Kent, we know from the beginning that Lear is "mad," that he is merely an "old man." Through Kent and even more through Cordelia, we know who Goneril and Regan really are; and, ironically, from Regan's own mouth we know Lear's trajectory from the beginning: "'Tis the infirmity of his age. *Yet he hath ever but slenderly known himself.*" *King Lear* shows us how this mad old man slowly and painfully, through old age and madness, reaches self-knowledge and the knowledge of his "loved ones" (in the sense of the Greek *philtatoi*), the world, and the essence of human beings. Slowly, in ever-widening circles, in a spiral coiling continuously back on self, Lear is to learn the truth he announced at the beginning, in words as ambiguous as those of Oedipus: how "dark" is his "purpose" and how very "burdened" he shall "crawl toward death."

Lear is set on the painful path toward recognition through confrontation with those around him. It is Kent, when he reappears, disguised, who tells him the truth. In answer to Lear's question, "What art thou?" he answers, "A man, sir," adding, "I do profess to be no less than I seem"; and this is the journey Lear now undertakes, from appearance to being (from "seems" to "is," in Hamlet's terms) to essential human being. The first level he must reach is that of the *tyrannos,* of "King." When, in the same scene, Lear again asks Kent, "What art thou?" he replies, "A very honest-hearted fellow, and as poor as the king." For a moment, Lear's reaction is of recognition and confession: "If thou be'st as poor for a subject as he's for a king, thou art poor enough." Slowly, talking to one of his knights, Lear realises the full extent of his ill-treatment at his daughters' hands, and with true Oedipal ambiguity announces what he will be doing for the rest of his life: "I will look further into 't." Lear has certainly "noted" that his Fool has "much pined away" since Cordelia left for France; the Fool then appears and, like Tiresias, makes a number of prophetic pronouncements: "Truth's a dog must to kennel; he must be whipped out, when the Lady Brach may stand by the fire and stink."

But Lear is no Oedipus. He listens to his "prophet" with increasing attention, because the germs of truth are already in him, as his exchanges with Kent and the knight show. "All" Lear has to do is become aware of this knowledge. Self-knowledge, as we saw, came for Oedipus from outside: he discovers his identity as if it were the object of an enquiry conducted by a third party. Lear must turn in on himself, dissect himself, and finally distinguish knowledge from awareness. Here "knowing oneself" is transposed into a Christian dimension: in Lear, the torture is internal from the start: in Oedipus's case only at the end, after recognition. Self-illusion is possible for Lear, but true *méconnaissance* and self-oblivion is not. He has to touch the bottom of self-awareness. It is hardly surprising that his "wits begin to turn": "madness" does, indeed, "that way lie." The text contains here a profound echo of the Christian ideal: "Let no man deceive himself. If any man among you seemeth to be wise in this world, let him become a fool, that he may be wise" (I Cor. 3, 18). Lear moves slowly toward the abyss, first "a fool" in name only, by the "title," as the Fool points out, he was born with, a man who had "little wit in [his] bald crown" when he gave away his "golden one"; one who, as Goneril urges on him, should make use of his "good wisdom" and who instead begins to know himself ever more "slenderly":

> Does any here know me? This is not Lear.
> Does Lear walk thus, speak thus? Where are his eyes?
> Either his notion weakens, his discernings
> Are lethargied—Ha! Waking? 'Tis not so!
> Who is it that can tell me who I am?

"Lear's shadow" is the Fool's answer to his disquieting question as to his identity (and not, significantly, his *seed*). And for all Lear's blustering to Goneril that he will be himself again, and again assume "the shape which thou dost think / I have cast off for ever," the way to nothingness (the same *mēden* as Oedipus's) and madness is now all too clearly signposted. His wit will indeed "go slipshods," and madness will be ready for him, in word and deed. "The reason why the seven stars are no more than seven is a pretty reason," the Fool insists, with another twist of his maieutic knife. "Because they are not eight?" Lear offers, to which the Fool rejoins: "Yes, indeed. Thou wouldst make a good fool." And again, when Lear rails at his daughters' monstrous ingratitude, the Fool comments: "If thou wert my Fool, nuncle, I'd have thee beaten for being old before thy time," adding, at Lear's puzzled "How's that?": "Thou shouldst not have been old before thou hadst been wise." "O let me not be mad, sweet heaven!" Lear's shadow finally cries, "Keep me in temper; I would not be mad!"

The *hysterica passio* rises to a crescendo over the groundswell of the Fool's prophecies of blind and wise men, great wheels, and tempests, a

seminal speech in which all the images of the play thicken into enigmas more opaque than those of the Delphic oracle, the pronouncements
of a Hamlet-versed Old Testament (and not Theban) Sphinx:

> We'll set thee to school to an ant to teach thee there's no labouring
> i'the winter. All that follow their noses are led by their eyes, but blind
> men; and there's not a nose among twenty but can smell him that's
> stinking. Let go thy hold when a great wheel runs down a hill, lest
> it break thy neck with following. But the great one that goes upward,
> let him draw thee after. When a wise man gives thee better coun-
> sel, give me mine again; I would have none but knaves follow it,
> since a fool gives it.

Faced with this welter of mystery and misery, Lear's heart will not
"down," and before his daughters' insistent "You should be ruled and
led / By some discretion that concerns your state / Better than you yourself," before Goneril's refusal to meet anything but the barest "need,"
Lear's heart finally breaks. "Do not make me mad," he implores Goneril,
bidding her farewell and qualifying his recognition of her as "my flesh,
my blood, my daughter" with the coda "Or rather a disease that's in my
flesh / Which I must needs call mine." He rejects, then, this *philia* in the
act of recognising it, and invokes patience while asking the gods for a
"noble anger," threatening his daughters with "the terrors of the earth."
In a wave of self-pity, he sees himself as "a poor old man / As full of grief
as age; wretched in both," but at the same time refuses to weep:

> No, I'll not weep:
> I have full cause of weeping, but this heart
> Shall break into a hundred thousand flaws
> Or ere I'll weep. O Fool! I shall go mad.

The storm is gathering. In the meantime we have been appalled spectators of Gloucester's deception, perpetrated by the bastard Edmund in
the name of Nature, and the transformation of Edgar into "the basest and
most poorest shape / That ever penury in contempt of man / Brought
near to beast." Edgar saves himself by becoming another, a beggar who
feigns madness, silencing his own nature to become the voice of nothingness. His father, however, takes his "perpendicular fall" into Edmund's

trap and, in a series of appalling ironies, recognises the disruption in nature, managing to distinguish between the unnatural anger of Lear the father toward his daughter Cordelia precisely in the moment he sees son revolt against father in the story of treason his bastard offspring invents against the natural.

When the storm breaks, Shakespeare guides Gloucester and Lear toward recognition in scenes which have no parallel in the whole of Western literature. Gloucester fails to recognise "Tom" even as his son, leading his blind father into shelter, addresses him as "thou happy father." He equally fails to recognise Kent in the precise moment he recognises his prescience: "he said it would be thus, poor banish'd man!" but sees in Lear's madness the onset of his own, commenting querulously: "Thou say'st the king grows mad; I'll tell thee, friend, / I am almost mad myself"; in Edgar's presence he expresses his love for him despite the plot against his life, grief which, he acknowledges, "hath crazed my wits." When his eyes are plucked out, when all is "dark and comfortless," then he learns the truth and is able to recognise: "Oh, my follies! Then Edgar was abused." Edgar, for his part, recognises his father while meditating that "To be worst, / The lowest and most dejected thing of fortune, / Stands still in esperance, lives not in fear. / The lamentable change is from the best; / The worst returns to laughter," words he is forced to retract the moment he sees his father. The blind Gloucester, recognising that he "stumbled when [he] saw" and that now, with no aim in view, he "want[s] no eyes," confesses to his disguised son: "Oh, dear son Edgar, / The food of thy abused father's wrath, / Might I but live to see thee in my touch, / I'ld say I had eyes again!"

Like Lear, Gloucester also has a more far-reaching epiphany of the nature of humanity. When speaking to Edgar, he recalls the mad beggar (Edgar/Tom) he had met the night before, in the storm; man, he had mused, was no more than a worm, and this had made him think of his son. While considering that this particular beggar must have some power of reason, "else he could not beg," Gloucester reaches a further, devastating recognition: "As flies to wanton boys are we to th' gods; / They kill us for their sport." Immediately afterward, when he realises that the beggar-companion guiding him to Dover is mad, his vision of the truth is further extended: "'Tis the times' plague, when madmen lead the blind." Formulating his desperate Weltanschauung, Gloucester thus crawls toward the "high and bending" cliff where he hopes to meet his death.

The sequence requires little comment. Recognition has become a universe in itself. Memory, mental association, presence, failed recognition, madness, and blindness all mesh into a strangling knot containing skeins of death, despair, and awareness both clearly visible and tragically, deliberately, confused. Recognition and reversal—*peripeteia*—break in wave after desperate wave. But what, then, is anagnorisis, this move from ignorance to awareness, in *King Lear?*

The beginnings of an answer lie in Lear's parallel path. In the storm of Act III, Lear, "a poor, infirm, weak and despised old man," veering between patience and anger, his brain loosening its grip, enters a long, tormented but inevitably downward spiral of knowledge. The obsession with filial ingratitude opens the way to madness and wisdom. The storm strikes flat the thick rotundity of the world, cracks nature's mould, and spills all germens that make ungrateful man, as Lear had asked it to; but the "contentious storm" and the "tempest in [his] mind" are the same thing, as Lear perceives in a lightning flash, so that the storm is striking flat the world and intellect as if they were identical, annulling reality and perception and cancelling out all the objects which fill a normal world, a normal mind. In cracking the moulds of nature, they level world and mind to two specular versions of a tabula rasa, on which the new, paradoxical wisdom of madness can etch elusive, fragmented signs of awareness and, particularly, flashes of understanding which, however, lead to no *saphēs,* no certain knowledge.

While Nature unleashes itself around him, Lear peels the old world like an onion: "undivulged crimes," "close pent-up guilts," perjury, filial ingratitude, kingship, justice, and female hearts which, in his grimly unmetaphoric referent, he wishes to "anatomize," in order to determine if "there [is] any cause in nature that makes [them] hard." He peels down to "the thing itself" which he perceives in Tom/Edgar, "unaccommodated man" who is "no more than but such a poor, bare, forked animal." Throwing off all "lendings," Lear becomes a new Job and grasps truth's core, the nothingness of *Oedipus the King:* "Is man no more than this?" It is this nakedness which makes him recognise, in Tom, his "philosopher," his "learned Theban" and "Athenian"—his Tiresias and Socrates—and in a mad drive for total knowledge, he asks: "What is the cause of thunder?" He is no longer able to think of what most harms him: caught between the inner and outer storm, he searches desperately for the original cause in nature, in Regan's heart, and in the thunder. But the moulds of nature are indeed cracked; only humanity is left, glimpsed through recognition, to be reconstructed from scratch, a temporary fragment, starting from the humblest element of sheer humble necessity. Hence Lear's concern for his Fool, for the "houseless poverty" of Poor Tom, and for all the "poor naked wretches" through whom a king, by accepting to share their condition and to experience their feelings personally, might build a world where to "show the heavens more just."

From this point on there is no letup in Lear's painful, painstaking process of re-cognition. When the storm has passed and the scene moves to Dover, all the threads of this complex plot come together. Gloucester and Edgar make their way toward what Gloucester believes to be the "fearful" and "dizzy" cliff he is seeking for. His guide's voice is "alter'd," Gloucester notes, but far from inducing recognition, the very same voice is able to fabricate the ultimate illusion: a vertiginous height, created in a welter of beetle-sized "crows and choughs," sampire gatherers, and fishermen no bigger than mice, from which he can tumble "perpendicularly" into the long-sought oblivion. Here, in a device which is to recur in a number of the later plays, Gloucester does indeed experience a sort of death and resurrection. After his 'fall' he meets a different Edgar, who exclaims at the miracle of his being alive, who calls him "father" for the first time, defines Tom as "some fiend," and, by arrogating the gods' ability to remedy "men's impossibilities"—in short, by constructing a parallel, verbal and deceptive, reality—gives him memory, a new self-awareness, and a new life: "I do remember now," Gloucester states. "Henceforth I'll bear / Affliction till it do cry out itself / 'Enough, enough,' and die." Or, as his son states at the end of the play, "Men must endure / Their going hence, even as their coming hither."

When the mad Lear reappears, Gloucester's catharsis—though not Lear's—is already over. The first of the recognition scenes now occurs, between Gloucester, who, in his blindness, has discovered some sort of reason, and Lear, who is still searching. The anagnorisis, here, is precisely this meeting and mixing of two states of awareness, or, as Edgar glosses Lear's comments in Act IV, "matter and impertinency mixed! / Reason in madness." While Gloucester recognises Lear almost immediately, on hearing his voice, Lear continues to grope his way toward the truth. Are we to take his "Ha! Goneril,—with a white beard!" as meaning he actually mistakes Gloucester for his daughter? What is his degree of awareness at this stage? When he answers Gloucester's question with an ironic, "Ay, every inch a king," and anathematises adultery, copulation, and "the sulphurous pit" of womanhood, Lear curiously mentions "Gloucester's bastard son" who "was kinder to his father than my daughters / Got 'tween lawful sheets." A moment later, when Gloucester attempts to kiss his hand, a further existential epiphany makes him respond, "Let me wipe it first; it smells of mortality." The entire exchange between the two old men is a counterpoint of personal obsessions, mutual empathy, and flashes of truth. "O ruin'd piece of nature!" Gloucester comments in his turn, with the voice of the Chorus in *Oedipus*: "This great world / Shall so wear out to nought." And when he goes on to ask, "Dost thou know me?" the recognition of Lear's answer is wonderfully oblique and oracular: "I remember thine *eyes* well enough." Lear's memory hones in on the very center of Gloucester's new awareness, of his new, painful existence: his eyes. And he never shifts his attention (or ours, or that of his addressee) until he has extracted some form of truth from the scene, bending Gloucester to the discourse of seeming madness: "Your eyes are in a heavy case, your purse in a light; yet you see how this world goes." "I see it feelingly," Gloucester replies, with an ambivalence worthy of Oedipus. But Lear both savages and caps his synaesthesia: "What, art mad? A man may see how this world goes with no eyes. Look with thine ears."

This is true knowledge and true wisdom. It needs no sense perception, no intellectual *gnōmē,* no syllogistic reasoning. Rather, it is based on experience and on the ability to extrapolate a parable from it and recognise truth within daily life: "Thou hast seen a farmer's dog bark at a beggar? And the creature run from the cur? There thou mightst behold the great image of authority; a dog's obeyed in office." Through all the apparent meanderings of his madness, Lear circles round the original goad, kingly power: the concept of justice is overturned and the ancient *tyrannos* absolves all his persecutors. But his tongue ever turns to aching tooth, the eyes. Finally, after near-unbearable cat-and-mouse retarding, he offers complete recognition: "If thou wilt weep my fortunes, take *my* eyes. / I know thee well enough; thy name is Gloucester." It is recognition which makes of Lear a "preaching" prophet, Oedipus and Chorus at once; which brings to light the deeper truth rooted in being human; which leads to re-cognition:

Thou must be patient; we came crying hither.
Thou *knowest* the first time that we smell the air
We wawl and cry. I will preach to thee—Mark!
[...]
When we are born we cry that we are come
To this great stage of fools.

In the following sequence, as Lear is hurried away to Cordelia's camp, Gloucester again asks Edgar, "Now, good sir, what are you." No recognition is yet possible, despite the clues of Edgar's poignant preceding line, "Well pray you, father." Yet Edgar answers with a significant statement, in which his "known and feeling sorrows" and the poverty that has made him "tame to fortune's blows," are not simply the reasons he is "pregnant to good pity" but are also, for the moment, the only real answers to the events of the play. Gloucester offers his own vision, however, echoing the rejection of awareness we have already heard in *Oedipus*. He blesses Lear's madness and praises folly, which keeps thought safely separate from pain:

The King is mad; how stiff is my wild sense,
That I stand up and have ingenious feeling
Of my huge sorrows! Better I were distract;
So should my thought be severed from my griefs,
And woes by wrong imagination lose
The knowledge of themselves . . .

But the king is far from mad and regains complete possession of himself in the following scene, when he recognises Cordelia. The way Shakespeare wakes Lear from his madness and restores him, purified, to an acceptance of life is one of the miracles of the theatre. The king's descent into madness and the concomitant growth of his wisdom had been slow and spasmodic; his resurrection looks swift by comparison, but Shakespeare is in no hurry and reaches the final recognition in a retarding which is all the more extraordinary for being concentrated in a very few lines. Cordelia addresses her father as a solicitous subject: "How does my royal lord? How fares your majesty?" The king's answer emerges from an abyss, suspended between his own hell and the heaven of his daughter:

> You do me wrong to take me out o' the' grave.
> Thou art a soul in bliss; but I am bound
> Upon a wheel of fire, that mine own tears
> Do scald like molten lead.

As the Fool's prophecy of the wheel is fulfilled, Lear sees Cordelia as a blessed soul, a breath of Paradise. Recognition momentarily moves beyond this world only to plunge back into exhausted flesh. Again, when she asks him, "Sir, do you know me?" he answers, "You are a spirit, I know; where did you die?" He then quickly regains a sense of time and space—"Where have I been? Where am I? Fair daylight?"—but nebulously, his sensorial perception still dulled: "I will not swear these are my hands," and even though he feels the pinprick he applies, he needs to be "assured of [his] condition." Cordelia then asks for his blessing, at which Lear kneels and, in twelve tentative, tormented lines gropingly completes his anagnorisis. He begins from the few sure facts of his age and his madness but fears he is not in his "perfect mind"; he thinks he should recognise Cordelia and Kent but is "doubtful"; realises he has lost the memory of self and the world because he has lost any notion of space, time, and the very clothes he wears; then, in a second's illumination, recognises his daughter at the instant he remembers he is (still, simply, but totally) a man:

> Pray, do not mock me:
> I am a very foolish fond old man,
> Fourscore and upward, not an hour more or less;
> And, to deal plainly,
> I fear I am not in my perfect mind.
> Methinks I should know you and know this man;
> Yet I am doubtful: for I am mainly ignorant
> What place this is, and all the skill I have
> Remembers not these garments; nor I know not
> Where I did lodge last night. Do not laugh at me;
> For as I am a man, I think this lady
> To be my child Cordelia.

Everything is suspended in the stupor of this beatific vision: memory and being, knowledge and existence, madness and wisdom. "Pray you now, forget and forgive," Lear asks her soon afterward. In this moment between past, present, and future, recognition means a new awareness, an openness toward another being. In sharp contrast with Lear's previous self-absorption, the (all too human) awareness of the wisdom of madness, this recognition, forged on a wheel of fire, is communion: a very human wisdom sublimated and purified by acceptance. Yet later, after their defeat, when Cordelia invites her father to see "these daughters and these sisters," his mind closes in on his prison, a cage into which the outside world penetrates only through the minds and sensations of the prisoners, through the exclusive perception of the self. Here the contemplating awareness will ultimately become recognition of the world within the self: a divine knowledge, as if one self communicating with another took on something of the Godhead: "as if we were God's spies." This is both humility and the taking upon oneself of what Lear defines as "the mystery of things": *not,* as Oedipus would propound, an enquiry into the nature of the mystery, but living, and praying, and singing, and the telling of old tales; a detached, smiling knowledge of natural and political reality, of the minutest, radiant details of being (the "gilded butterflies") and the seesaw of becoming (the "court news" learnt from "poor rogues"); "sacrifices" upon which "the gods themselves throw incense."

This is the knowledge which will cast its aura over Shakespeare's last plays, in the miraculous scenes of recognition between father and daughter or husband and wife in *Cymbeline, Pericles,* and *The Winter's Tale,* and which from Lear's tempest leads almost directly to *The Tempest.* In *King Lear* this divine and human wisdom remains, however, imprisoned and condemned, as it were, just as in *Oedipus the King* it prefigures the transformation to take place in *Oedipus at Colonus.*

The scenes of recognition which follow that between Lear and Cordelia throw all the hard-achieved, momentary equilibrium out of joint, inexorably moving in quite another direction. The first is a tragic version of the revelation of the unknown knight in medieval romance. Edgar, no longer dressed as Poor Tom, appears at the third sound of the trumpet, challenges Edmund, and mortally wounds him. Significantly, Edgar's name—"lost, / By treason's tooth bare-gnawn and canker-bit"— is only revealed when Edmund confesses his sins, leading to a *quasi-*religious recognition between the two half brothers. "The gods are just, and of our pleasant vices / Make instruments to plague us," Edgar states, pointing the moral of divine *contrapasso,* while Edmund extends the play's wheel image: "Th' hast spoken right; 'tis true; / The wheel is come full circle; I am here."

Edmund's recognition of his brother ends in the sense of "right" which he intends to honour "despite of [his] own nature": through his death, and in a last-minute attempt to revoke his order and save Lear's and Cordelia's life. Edgar's exposure of Edmund only occurs, however, when he has revealed himself to his father. This revelation kills Gloucester, whose "flaw'd heart, / Alack, too weak the conflict to support! / 'Twixt two extremes of passion, joy and grief, / Burst smilingly." Again, knowledge leads to death, here direct and physical. Emotions can kill. And although this is a smiling death of reconciliation, Lear still has to plummet from the peak of the infinite "mystery of things" where supreme knowledge and boundless ignorance may meet to the small, appalling, individual knowledge of his daughter's death. In a return to things of the earth, since "death" and "earth" are synonyms, knowledge here is absolute, an all too obvious, certain *saphēs:* "I know when one is dead and when one lives; / She's dead as earth."

When, in the play's last recognition scene, Lear, through his "dull sight," recognises Kent, the knowledge is now useless. "I'll see that straight," Lear murmurs when Kent tries to reveal himself as the very man who had followed him as his long-disguised servant. Lear bids him welcome, but, as Albany remarks, "he knows not what he sees." His death approaches. "All's cheerless, dark and deadly," Kent now recognises. The whole process of passing from ignorance to knowledge, the multiple, layered *peripeteia* of recognition are no longer of any significance. Spectators and readers, drained by a plot of unrelenting bleakness after it had promised peace and transfiguration, are by the end of the play less than "the thing itself": even poorer, barer, and more desperately bereft than after the annihilation of Oedipus. All we learn is that if, in Edgar's words, "The oldest hath borne most," "We that are young / Shall never see so much, nor live so long," and almost envy Kent his "journey shortly to go" after his master, since our own has ended so devastatingly. Shakespeare has not "improved" Sophocles' invention: indeed, he knew nothing of it. He has made no attempt at the delayed-action mechanism of *Oedipus*. What he has done is to smash the clock of knowledge and set off a series of explosions, each more terrifying than the one before, building up a cataclysmic storm. In other words, he has effected a terrifying transmigration, from pagan to Christian civilisation, of the *telos* of Western knowledge: nothingness.

Bibliography

The bibliography is meant to enable the reader to track the texts discussed in the book and to follow my argument. It is by no means exhaustive but rather selective and slightly idiosyncratic.

1. Electra and Hamlet: Recognition and Reasoning

I have used the three Greek Electra plays in the following editions: *Aeschyli Septem Quae Supersunt Tragoediae,* ed. G. Murray, London, 1955; Euripides, *Les Troyennes, Iphigénie en Tauride, Electre,* texte établi et traduit par L. Parmentier et H. Gregoire, Paris, 1968; Sophocles, *Electra,* ed. J. H. Kells, Cambridge, 1973. The English translations are from Aeschylus, *The Oresteian Tragedy,* trans. P. Vellacott, Harmondsworth, 1956; Euripides, *Medea and Other Plays,* trans. P. Vellacott, Harmondsworth, 1963; Sophocles, *Electra. Women of Trachis. Philoctetes. Ajax,* trans. E. F. Watling, Harmondsworth, 1953. W. Shakespeare, *Hamlet,* ed. H. Jenkins, London and New York, 1982, is the text on which I base my study. The other texts employed in the discussion are V. Alfieri, *Oreste. Opere,* vol. I, ed. A. Di Benedetto, Milan and Naples, 1977; Aristophanes, *Frogs,* ed. and trans. B. B. Rogers, Cambridge, Mass., 1974; P. Corneille, *Oeuvres complètes,* vol. IV, Paris, 1838; J. Giraudoux, *Electre,* Paris, 1937; J. W. von Goethe, *Wilhelm Meisters Lehrjahre,* vol. VII, *Hamburger Ausgabe,* ed. E. Trunz, Hamburg, 1948–64; H. von Hofmannsthal, *Elektra, Gesammelte Werke,* vol. V, *Dramen,* Berlin, 1924; J. Joyce, *Ulysses,* Harmondsworth, 1969; R. Lowell, *The Oresteia of Aeschylus,* London, 1979; E. O'Neill, *Mourning Becomes Electra: Nine Plays,* New York, 1941; J. P. Sartre, *Les Mouches,* ed. R. J. North, London, 1963; Voltaire, *Oreste. Oeuvres complètes,* vol. I, Paris, 1827; S. Weil, *Intuitions Pré-Chrétiennes,* Paris, 1951; M. Yourcenar, *Electre. Théatre,* vol. II, Paris, 1971.

I have consulted the following editions and commentaries of Aristotle's *Poetics: Dell'Arte Poetica,* ed. C. Gallavotti, Milan, 1974; *Poetics,* ed. D. W. Lucas, Oxford, 1968; G. F. Else, *Aristotle's Poetics: The Argument,* Cambridge, Mass., 1957; *La Poétique,* texte, traduction, notes par R. Dupont-Roc et J. Lallot, Paris, 1980; L. Castelvetro, *Poetica d'Aristotele volgarizzata e sposta,* ed. W. Romani, Bari, 1978–79; H. J. Pye, *A Commentary Illustrating the Poetic of Aristotle by Examples Chiefly Taken from the Modern Poets,* London, 1792.

On the problem of recognition in general, and the way in which I examine it in the light of the *Poetics,* I refer the reader to T. Cave, *Recognitions: A Study in Poetics,* Oxford, 1988; F. Kermode, *The Art of Telling,* Cambridge, Mass., 1983; G. Wunberg, *Wiedererkennen,* Tübingen, 1983; to my *The Tragic and the Sublime in Medieval Literature,* Cambridge, 1989, and *The Bible and Its Rewritings,* Oxford, 1999; to G. Else, *Plato and Aristotle on Poetry,* ed. P. Burian, Chapel Hill and London, 1986; V. Goldschmidt, *Temps physique et temps tragique chez Aristote,* Paris, 1982; S. Goldhill, *The Poet's Voice: Essays on Poetics and Greek Literature,* Cambridge, 1991; S. Goldhill, *Reading Greek Tragedy,* Cambridge, 1986; T. Gould, *The Ancient Quarrel between Poetry and Philosophy,* Princeton, 1990; S. Halliwell, *Aristotle's Poetics,* London, 1986; M. Heath, *The Poetics of Greek Tragedy,* London, 1987; J. Jones, *On Aristotle and Greek Tragedy,* London, 1962; F. L. Lucas, *Tragedy: Serious Drama in Relation to Aristotle's Poetics,* London, 1957; A. O. Rorty, ed., *Essays on Aristotle's Poetics,* Princeton, 1992.

I refer readers to the bibliography of chapter 5 for general works on Greek tragedy. It would be impossible to offer even selected readings on Aeschylus, Sophocles, and Euripides, and I therefore list here only some of those studies which have influenced my argument in this chapter: B. Snell, *Aischylos und das Handeln im Drama,* Leipzig, 1928; S. Goldhill, *Language, Sexuality, Narrative: The Oresteia,* Cambridge, 1984; A. Martina, *Il riconoscimento di Oreste nelle Coefore e nelle due Elettre,* Rome, 1975; B. M. W. Knox, *The Heroic Temper: Studies in Sophoclean Tragedy,* Berkeley and Los Angeles, 1964; R. P. Winnington-Ingram, *Sophocles: An Interpretation,* Cambridge, 1980; C. Segal, *Tragedy and Civilization: An Interpretation of Sophocles,* Cambridge, Mass., 1981; C. Segal, *Sophocles' Tragic World: Divinity, Nature, Society,* Cambridge, Mass., and London, 1995; M. Untersteiner, *Sofocle,* Milan, 1974; G. Paduano, *La formazione del mondo ideologico e poetico di Euripide,* Pisa, 1968; G. Paduano, *Il nostro Euripide l'umano,* Florence, 1986; P. Vellacott, *Ironic Drama: A Study of Euripides' Method and Meaning,* Cambridge, 1975.

On the transition from Greek drama to Shakespeare and the moderns, I recommend A. Poole, *Tragedy: Shakespeare and the Greek Example,* Oxford, 1987; N. D'Agostino, *Shakespeare e i Greci,* Rome, 1994; J. Kerrigan, *Revenge Tragedy: Aeschylus to Armageddon,* Oxford, 1996; K. Hamburger, *Von Sophokles zu Sartre,* Stuttgart, 1962. For an example of thematic reading, G. Steiner, *Antigones,* Oxford, 1984.

Literature on *Hamlet* and Shakespearean drama is even more vast than that on Greek tragedy. I cite here only the basic works that have helped me shape this chapter. On Shakespeare in general, A. C. Bradley, *Shakespearean Tragedy,* London, 1905; G. Wilson Knight, *The Wheel of Fire: Interpretations of Shakespearian Tragedy,* London, 1949; G. Wilson Knight, *The Imperial Theme,* London, 1951; E. M. W. Tillyard, *Shakespeare's Problem Plays,* London, 1950; M. C. Bradbrook, *Shakespeare and Elizabethan Poetry,* London, 1951; M. C. Bradbrook, *Themes and Conventions in Elizabethan Tragedy,* Cambridge, 1953; T. Spencer, *Shakespeare and the Nature of Man,* New York, 1959; K. Muir, *Shakespeare's Tragic Sequence,* London, 1972; W. Clemen, *The Development of Shakespeare's Imagery,* London, 1977; R. Weimann, *Shakespeare and the Popular Tradition in the Theater,* ed. R. Schwartz, Baltimore and London, 1978; R. Marienstras, *Le Proche et le lointain,* Paris, 1981; C. Belsey, *The Subject of Tragedy: Identity and Difference in Renaissance Drama,* London, 1985; *Shakespeare. La nostalgia dell'essere,* ed. A. Serpieri, Parma, 1985; D. Mehl, *Shakespeare's Tragedies: An Introduction,* Engl. trans., Cambridge, 1986; S. Greenblatt, *Shakespearean Negotiations,* Berkeley, 1987; M. Evans, *Signifying Nothing: Truth's True Contents in Shakespeare's Texts,* Athens, Ga., 1989; A. Lombardo, *Per una critica imperfetta,* Rome, 1992; G. Melchiori, *Shakespeare. Genesi e struttura delle opere,* Bari, 1994. On *Hamlet* in particular: G. de Santillana, H. von Dechend, *Hamlet's Mill,* Boston, 1983; I. Gollancz, *The Sources of Hamlet,* London, 1926; C. S. Lewis, *Hamlet: The Prince or the Poem?* London, 1943; E. Jones, *Hamlet and Oedipus,* London, 1949; C. H. C. Williamson, ed., *Readings on the Character of Hamlet,* London, 1950; D. G. James, *The Drama of Learning,* London, 1951; C. Schmitt, *Hamlet oder Hekuba,* Düsseldorf and Köln, 1956; P. Alexander, *Hamlet Father and Son,* London, 1955; L. C. Knights, *An Approach to Hamlet,* London, 1960; A. Gurr, *Hamlet and the Distracted Globe,* Edinburgh, 1978; L. C. Knights, *Hamlet and Other Shakespearean Essays,* Cambridge, 1978; V. Gentili, *La recita della follia. Funzioni dell'insania nel teatro dell'età di Shakespeare,* Turin, 1978; M. Scofield, *The Ghosts of Hamlet: The Play and Modern Writers,* Cambridge, 1980; A. Green, *Hamlet et Hamlet. Une interprétation psychanalytique de la représentation,* Paris, 1982; H. Bloom, ed., *Shakespeare's Hamlet: Modern Critical Interpretations,* New York, 1986; H. Gatti, *The Renaissance Drama of Knowledge,* London, 1989; *Hamlet dal testo alla scena,* ed. M. Tempera, Bologna, 1990; *Ombre di un'ombra. Amleto e i suoi fantasmi,* ed. L. Curti, Naples, 1994. Now I would also refer readers to S. Greenblatt, *Hamlet in Purgatory,* Princeton, 2001.

2. *In gentil hertes ay redy to repaire:* Francesca and Troilus

The primary texts for this chapter are the following: *The Complete Poems of John Keats,* ed. M. Allott, London, 1970; for Guinizzelli, *Poeti del Duecento,* ed.

G. Contini, Milan and Naples, 1960; Boethius, *Tractates, De Consolatione Philosophiae,* London and Cambridge, Mass., 1973; Dante, *Commedia,* ed. A. M. Chiavacci Leonardi, 3 vols., Milan, 1991–97; Dante, *Opere Minori,* voll. I, 1–2 e II, Milan and Naples, 1979–88; *Dante's Lyric Poetry,* ed. K. Foster and P. Boyde, Oxford, 1967; *Tutte le opere di Giovanni Boccaccio,* ed. V. Branca, vol. I, Milan, 1964; *The Riverside Chaucer,* gen. ed. L. D. Benson, Boston, 1987; G. Chaucer, *Troilus & Criseyde: A New Edition of 'The Book of Troilus,'* ed. B. A. Windeatt, London, 1984.

As for critical material, I limit myself here to mention only what is directly relevant to my argument: H. Rey-Flaud, *La névrose courtoise,* Paris, 1983; D. S. Avalle, *Ai Luoghi di Delizia Pieni,* Milan and Naples, 1977; V. Moleta, *Guinizelli in Dante,* Rome, 1980; T. Barolini, *Dante's Poets: Textuality and Truth in the "Comedy,"* Princeton, 1984; A. M. Chiavacci Leonardi, *La guerra de la pietate. Saggio per un'interpretazione dell'Inferno di Dante,* Naples, 1979; G. Contini, "Dante come personaggio-poeta della *Commedia,*" now in *Un'idea di Dante,* Turin, 1976; P. Dronke, "L'amor che move il sole e l'altre stelle," now in his *The Medieval Poet and His World,* Rome, 1984; P. Dronke, *Dante's Second Love: The Originality and the Contexts of the Convivio,* Exeter-Leeds, 1997; P. Dronke, "'Andreas Capellanus,'" now in his *Sources of Inspiration: Studies in Literary Transformations,* Rome, 1997; F. Ferrucci, *Il poema del Desiderio. Poetica e passione in Dante,* Milan, 1990; K. Foster, *God's Tree,* London, 1957; K. Foster, *The Two Dantes,* London, 1977; S. Kay, "Courts, Clerks, and Courtly Love," in *The Cambridge Companion to Medieval Romance,* ed. R. L. Krueger, Cambridge, 2000; E. D. Kirk, "Paradis Stood Formed in Hire Yen: Courtly Love and Chaucer's Re-vision of Dante," in *Acts of Interpretation: Essays in Medieval and Renaissance Literature in Honor of E. Talbot Donaldson,* ed. M. J. Carruthers and E. D. Kirk, Norman, Okla., 1982; C. S. Lewis, *The Allegory of Love: A Study in Medieval Tradition,* London, 1936; J. Mann, *Geoffrey Chaucer,* Hemel Hempstead, 1991 (I am very grateful to Jill Mann for having allowed me to read and draw upon her unpublished "Lectura Dantis" on *Inferno* V); A. J. Smith, *The Methaphysics of Love,* Cambridge, 1985; J. M. Steadman, *Disembodied Laughter: Troilus and the Apotheosis Tradition,* Berkeley, 1972; K. Taylor, *Chaucer Reads "The Divine Comedy,"* Stanford, 1989; W. Wetherbee, *Chaucer and the Poets: An Essay on Troilus and Criseyde,* Ithaca, N.Y., 1984. The theme of Troilus from antiquity to the Middle Ages and modernity is treated in *The European Tragedy of Troilus,* Oxford, 1989, ed. P. Boitani. I have indirectly touched on some aspects of the transitions examined in this chapter in my *The Tragic and the Sublime in Medieval Literature,* Cambridge, 1989.

3. The Genius to Improve an Invention: Transformations of the *Knight's Tale*

The primary texts for this chapter are G. Boccaccio, *Teseida,* ed. A. Limentani in vol. I of *Tutte le opere, cit.,* Milan, 1964; *The Riverside Chaucer, cit.; The Two Noble*

Kinsmen, ed. N. W. Bawcutt, Harmondsworth, 1977; *The Two Noble Kinsmen,* New York, 1966; *Teatro completo di William Shakespeare,* vol. VI, *I drammi romanzeschi,* ed. G. Melchiori (with an important introduction to *The Two Noble Kinsmen*), Milan, 1981; J. Kinsley, ed., *The Poems of John Dryden,* vol. IV, Oxford, 1958. With the majority of modern critics I believe that in *The Two Noble Kinsmen* the entire Act I; II, i; III, i; III, ii (?); and the whole of Act V (with the exception of scene ii) are by Shakespeare.

I mention only the critical material which has contributed to shape my discussion: H. Cooper, "The Girl with Two Lovers: Four Canterbury Tales," in *Medieval Studies for J. A. W. Bennett,* ed. P. L. Heyworth, Oxford, 1981; E. T. Donaldson, *The Swan at the Well: Shakespeare Reading Chaucer,* New Haven and London, 1980; P. Edwards, "On the Design of *The Two Noble Kinsmen,*" now in the Signet edition of the play, edited by C. Leech, *cit.; Il Boccaccio nella Cultura Inglese e Americana,* ed. G. Galigani, Florence, 1974; T. J. Hatton, "Medieval Anticipations of Dryden's Stylistic Revolution: *The Knight's Tale,*" *Language and Style,* 7 (1974); W. Juneman, *Drydens Fabeln und ihre Quellen,* Britannica 5, Hamburg, 1932; A. Middleton, "The Modern Art of Fortifying: *Palamon and Arcite* as Epicurean Epic," *Chaucer Review,* 3 (1968); E. Miner, *Dryden's Poetry,* Bloomington and London, 1967; E. Miner, "Chaucer in Dryden's *Fables,*" in *Studies in Criticism and Aesthetics 1660–1800,* ed. H. Anderson and J. S. Shea, Minneapolis, 1967; J. Sloman, "An Interpretation of Dryden's *Fables,*" *Eighteenth-Century Studies,* 4 (1971); J. Sloman, *Dryden: The Poetics of Translation,* ed. A. McWhir, Toronto, 1985; T. Spencer, "The *Two Noble Kinsmen,*" now in the Signet edition of the play, *cit.;* A. Thompson, *Shakespeare's Chaucer: A Study in Literary Origins,* Liverpool, 1978; W. H. Williams, "*Palamon and Arcite* and the *Knight's Tale,*" *Modern Language Review,* 9 (1914).

4. *Are you here?* Brunetto, Dante, and Eliot

Primary texts for this chapter are canto XV of the *Inferno* in A. M. Chiavacci Leonardi's edition, *cit.,* and T. S. Eliot's *Four Quartets* in *The Complete Poems and Plays,* London, 1969. I also mention and quote from T. S. Eliot, *Tradition and the Individual Talent* (1917), in *Selected Prose of T. S. Eliot,* ed. F. Kermode, London, 1975; T. S. Eliot, *Note sur Mallarmé et Poe,* French trans. R. Fernandez, *Nouvelle Revue Française,* 1 November 1926; T. S. Eliot, *Dante* (1929), London, 1965; T. S. Eliot, "What Dante Means to Me," in his *To Criticize the Critic,* New York, 1965 (and see T. S. Eliot, *The Varieties of Metaphysical Poetry,* ed. R. Schuchard, London, 1993); *The Inferno of Dante Alighieri,* London and New York, Temple Classics, 1970 reprint, from which all English translations of Dante in this chapter are taken; S. Mallarmé, *Oeuvres complètes. Poésies,* Paris, 1983; Virgil,

144   Bibliography

Eneide, ed. E. Paratore, Milan, 1978–83 (English translations from the *Aeneid* are Dryden's).

Criticism includes the following: on Dante, E. Auerbach, *Dante als Dicther der irdischen Welt,* Berlin and Leipzig, 1929, Engl. trans. R. Manheim as *Dante, Poet of the Secular World,* Chicago and London, 1961; A. Pézard, *Dante sous la pluie de feu. Enfer, chant XV,* Paris, 1951; F. Montanari, "Brunetto Latini," *Cultura e scuola,* 4 (1965); F. Salsano, "Il canto XV dell'Inferno," in his *La coda di Minosse,* Milan, 1968; C. Segre in *Lectura Dantis neapolitana. Inferno,* Naples, 1980; on Eliot, J. A.W. Bennett, "*Little Gidding,* a Poem of Pentecost," in his *The Humane Medievalist,* ed. P. Boitani, Rome, 1982; H. Blamires, *Word Unheard: A Guide through Eliot's Four Quartets,* London, 1969; R. L. Brett, *Reason and Imagination,* Oxford, 1960; A. M. Charity, "T. S. Eliot: The Dantean Recognitions," in *The Waste Land in Different Voices,* ed. A. D. Moody, London, 1974; H. Gardner, *The Composition of Four Quartets,* London, 1978; R. MacCallum, *Time Lost and Regained: The Theme of Eliot's Quartets,* Toronto, 1953; C. Ricks, "A Note on *Little Gidding,*" *Essays in Criticism,* 25 (1975); in general, F. Kermode, *The Genesis of Secrecy,* Cambridge, Mass., 1979; on the Dante-Eliot relationship, M. Praz, "T. S. Eliot and Dante," in his *The Flaming Heart,* New York, 1958; L. Unger, *Eliot's Compound Ghost: Influence and Confluence,* University Park, Pa., 1981; S. Y. McDougal, "T. S. Eliot's Metaphysical Dante," in *Dante among the Moderns,* ed. S. Y. McDougal, Chapel Hill, 1985; D. Manganiello, *T. S. Eliot and Dante,* London, 1989.

5. Oedipus and Lear: Recognition and Nothingness

The two central texts for this chapter are Sophocles, *Oedipus Rex,* ed. R. D. Dawe, Cambridge, 1982 (English trans. by D. Grene, in D. Grene and R. Lattimore, eds., *Greek Tragedies,* vol. I, Chicago, 1960); and Shakespeare, *King Lear,* ed. K. Muir, London, 1969 reprint, accompanied by *Re Lear,* ed. G. Melchiori, Milan, 1976.

The most important studies on Greek tragedy and Sophocles are K. Reinhardt, *Sophocles,* Engl. trans., Oxford, 1979; E. R. Dodds, *The Greeks and the Irrational,* Berkeley and Los Angeles, 1951; T. Woodard, ed., *Sophocles: A Collection of Critical Essays,* Englewood Cliffs, N.J., 1966; H. D. F. Kitto, *Poiesis,* Berkeley, 1966; B. Vickers, *Towards Greek Tragedy: Drama, Myth, Society,* London, 1973; J. M. Bremer, *Hamartia: Tragic Error in the Poetics,* Amsterdam, 1968; J. Ferguson, *A Companion to Greek Tragedy,* Austin, 1972; J.-P. Vernant and P. Vidal-Naquet, *Mythe et tragédie en Grèce ancienne,* Paris, 1976; S. Said, *La faute tragique,* Paris, 1978; M. Detienne, *Les maîtres de vérité en Grèce archaïque,* Paris, 1967; O. Taplin, *Greek Tragedy in Action,* Berkeley, 1978; *Oxford Readings in Greek*

Tragedy, ed. E. Segal, Oxford, 1983; V. Di Benedetto, *Sofocle,* Florence, 1983; C. Segal, *Interpreting Greek Tragedy: Myth, Poetry, Text,* Ithaca, N.Y., 1986; J.-P. Vernant and P. Vidal-Naquet, *Mythe et tragédie deux,* Paris, 1986; M. C. Nussbaum, *The Fragility of Goodness,* Cambridge, 1986.

On *Oedipus Rex:* B. M. W. Knox, *Oedipus at Thebes,* New Haven, 1957; C. Lévi-Strauss, *Structural Antropology,* Engl. trans., Garden City, N.Y., 1967; E. R. Dodds, "On Misunderstanding the Oedipus Rex," *Greece and Rome,* 13 (1966); C. Diano, "Edipo figlio della Tyche," in *Saggezza e poetiche degli antichi,* Vicenza, 1968; D. A. Hester, "Oedipus and Jonah," *Proceedings of the Cambridge Philological Association,* 23 (1977); A. Cameron, *The Identity of Oedipus the King,* New York, 1965; P. Vellacott, *Sophocles and Oedipus,* London, 1971; D. I. Grossvogel, *Mystery and Its Fictions: From Oedipus to Agatha Christie,* Baltimore, 1978; A. Green, *The Tragic Effect: The Oedipus Complex in Tragedy,* Engl. trans., Cambridge, 1979; K. Reinhardt, *Sophocles,* Engl. trans., 3d ed., Oxford, 1977; M. Vegetti, *Tra Edipo e Euclide. Forme del sapere antico,* Milan, 1983; B. Gentili and A. Prestagostini, eds., *Edipo: Il teatro greco e la cultura europea,* Rome, 1986; J. Scherer, *Dramaturgies d'Oedipe,* Paris, 1987; *The Oedipus Papers,* ed. G. H. Pollock and J. M. Ross, Madison, 1988; P. Pucci, *Oedipus and the Fabrication of the Father: Oedipus Tyrannos in Modern Criticism and Philosophy,* Baltimore, 1992; T. Halter, *König Oedipus. Von Sophokles zu Cocteau,* Stuttgart, 1997; C. Segal, *Oedipus Tyrannus: Tragic Heroism and the Limits of Knowledge,* 2d ed., New York, 2001; and finally G. Paduano's splendid *Lunga storia di Edipo Re,* Turin, 1994.

On Shakespeare and *King Lear:* W. Empson, *The Structure of Complex Words,* London, 1931; E. H. Kantorowicz, *The King's Two Bodies,* Princeton, 1957; N. Frye, *Fools of Time,* London, 1967; J. F. Danby, *Shakespeare's Doctrine of Nature: A Study of King Lear,* London, 1959; N. Brooke, *Shakespeare: King Lear,* London, 1963; T. Hawkes, *Shakespeare and the Reason,* London, 1964; W. R. Elton, *King Lear and the Gods,* San Marino, Calif., 1966; P. A. Jorgensen, *Lear's Self-Discovery,* Berkeley, 1967; S. Cavell, "The Ambivalence of Love: A Reading of King Lear," in *Must We Mean What We Say?* New York, 1969; F. Kermode, ed., *King Lear: A Casebook,* London, 1969; S. L. Goldberg, *An Essay on King Lear,* Cambridge, 1974; M. Pagnini, *Shakespeare e il paradigma della specularità,* Pisa, 1976; P. Gullì Pugliatti, *I segni latenti. Scrittura come virtualità scenica in King Lear,* Messina and Florence, 1976; M. M. Hills, *Time, Space and Structure in King Lear,* Salzburg, 1976; A. Johnson, *Readings of Antony and Cleopatra and King Lear,* Pisa, 1979; R. Mullini, *Corruttore di parole. Il fool nel teatro di Shakespeare,* Bologna, 1983; *King Lear dal testo alla scena,* ed. M. Tempera, Bologna, 1986; S. Bassnett, *Shakespeare: The Elizabethan Plays,* London, 1993.

Index

The use of **bold** indicates coverage of a complete chapter.

147